Sona

The Story of a Dog Who Taught Me About Love

By
Ponchitta Pierce

Copyright © 2021 by Ponchitta Pierce

All rights reserved. No part of this publication may be reproduced, distributed or transmitted in any form or by any means, without prior written permission.

Publisher: Central Park South Publishing
Website: www.centralparksouthpublishing.com
Publisher's Note: True Story. This is a work of non-fiction.
Book Layout & Design: Mark Mázers
Cover: Mark Mázers
Sona by Ponchitta Pierce - 1st ed.

ISBN 978-1-956452-02-0

"Animals are such agreeable friends. They ask no questions, they pass no criticisms"- English novelist George Eliot

"Dogs are better than human beings because they know but do not tell" - American poet Emily Dickinson

"Some of my best leading men have been dogs and horses" - American actress Elizabeth Taylor

Central Park South Publishing

ALSO BY PONCHITTA PIERCE:

Keep Going No Matter What: The Reginald F. Lewis Legacy 20 Years Later

DEDICATION

To my mother Nora Vincent Pierce.
To Sona who made such a difference in my life.
To all those who helped me become the person I am.

Contents

Introduction 1
Chapter 1: How a Cocker Spaniel Changed My Life .. 3
Chapter 2: A Mind of His Own 19
Chapter 3: A Star is Born...................... 37
Chapter 4: It Takes an Urban Village 49
Chapter 5: The Animal Medical Center 61
Chapter 6: "Age Is Not a Disease"................ 73
Chapter 7: Keeping Your Dog Fit and Trim 89
Chapter 8: Help for Aging Dogs 101
Chapter 9: "Don't Worry, Your Dog Will
Show You How" 115
Chapter 10: When It's Time to Say Goodbye...... 127
Chapter 11: Moving On 141
Epilogue...................................... 153
About The Author 157
Acknowledgements 159

Introduction

When New York journalist Ponchitta Pierce brought an irresistible Cocker Spaniel puppy into her life, she had no idea what she was in for. At first, no one in Ponchitta's world was pleased about it. But this puppy had a face you could not forget, a personality that refused to be ignored, and knew exactly how to win over hearts.

It wasn't long before Ponchitta's assistant, her friends, the doormen downstairs, her mother, and even her boyfriend—who gave him his Hindi name, Sona—all fell in love with the new arrival.

They also soon found out that Sona got away with everything. He began to rule Ponchitta's day, edging her over on the bed, accompanying her on her travels to her boyfriend's home in Greenwich, Connecticut, and coming up with all kinds of antics to get her attention (he loved running with toilet paper), even while Ponchitta was on deadline! But Sona also had many medical challenges, not uncommon in dogs that have been inbred too much. Soon, Ponchitta and Sona had to face them as well.

In this heartfelt story of the love between a sly, clever dog and a very busy journalist, Ponchitta includes important, well-researched advice on raising a dog, tackling everything from training, feeding, and looking after a puppy to handling medical situations, insurance, aging, and, ultimately, the grieving process.

The result is a unique and insightful book that will make dog lovers laugh and cry but that is also a must-read for anyone thinking of bringing some puppy love into their life.

- 1 -

How a Cocker Spaniel Changed My Life

My friends had been telling me for years that I should buy a dog, but I'd always resisted the temptation. After all, I often thought, I probably needed more care than a puppy! Who was going to feed, walk, and spoil me? One day when I went for a walk on Manhattan's Upper East Side, I passed two windows of a popular pet shop on Lexington Avenue. In one of the windows, a very cute Cocker Spaniel puppy was lying down and gnawing on a chew toy. I smiled, passed the window, then stopped dead in my tracks. Curious, I turned around and walked back. Don't fall for that doggie in the window, I warned myself. Yet Cocker Spaniels were a special weakness of mine. "No harm in checking it out," I said aloud.

I went inside and asked the man working in the pet shop if I could hold the Cocker Spaniel. He separated the dog from his chew toy long enough to put the puppy in my arms, showing me how to correctly hold the puppy with my hand and arm supporting its chest. Once the dog was in my arms, I was smitten. I felt instant kinship! The dog's feelings? Maybe not so much. Yes, he licked and kissed me in earnest, but when he grew tired of my fawning attention, he started to squirm. The counter had a cutout area where puppies could be placed once they had met potential owners, so I set the dog down. Free once more, the puppy ignored me as he lay down. I wondered how many other people had marched into the store and asked to hold him. Maybe the puppy was used to being petted and held, and then watching people walk away.

Not so fast, I told myself as I gazed at the puppy with a longing that was palpable. Yet I loved the fact that when I was holding him, he'd seemed so confident and assured, rare in a puppy of his age. This probably meant he wouldn't need 24-hour attention, that he could entertain himself and wouldn't fear being alone. He seemed to sense there was a time for companionship and a time for solitude. In addition, he was a lovely shade of brown, had unbelievably large paws that were totally out of proportion to his size, floppy ears and deep liquid eyes, and a face that made you want to say, "Oh, baby!"

All of this added up to one inevitable conclusion. "I'll take him," I said. I hadn't discussed the idea of getting a dog with my boyfriend, or my assistant, or my mother, who was visiting from New Orleans. When I reached my apartment door, I tucked the dog under my coat, suddenly feeling guilty and self-conscious, especially because I'd just paid a princely sum for him. I tried to slip quickly into the apartment without a fuss. But Ajit Hutheesing, my boyfriend, spotted me almost instantly. He set down his newspaper and raised his eyebrows at me. "What's that?" he asked. And then, as reality hit him, he said, "I don't want another dog! I still haven't gotten over losing Shane."

I knew that not having Shane around had been difficult for Ajit. He probably didn't want to open himself up to a new pet because he didn't want to face the possibility of any additional loss. I scratched my new dog behind his ears.

My mother, Nora Pierce, was sitting in the living room listening to Ray Charles. She stood up from her chair and frowned. "I hate to ask," she said, "but who's going to take care of it?" I was, of course. I took care of all the dogs I had while growing up.

My eyes moved to my assistant, Maria Nikolakopoulos, who was sorting through papers on my desk. She looked alarmed at the sight of the dog and muttered something about quitting. I thought she was kidding, but I couldn't tell for sure. When I took the dog over to meet her, Maria stood stiffly and didn't seem to know how to pet a dog. "Like this," I said, as I took her hand, and placed it on the puppy's head. "Now rub gently."

Because Maria trusted me, she did as I instructed, although I couldn't tell from the expression on her face how comfortable she was.

"Don't worry, everyone," I announced. "I'll take care of him."

I set the puppy down. He sniffed around the sofa and then peed on the floor. I smiled sheepishly. "I'm sure he's just nervous," I said.

After a few hours, Ajit said, "Let's keep him for a week, and if it doesn't work out, we can return him."

A dog isn't like a coat that doesn't fit, I thought, but what I said was, "I know it's going to work. I promise!" Then I kissed both him and the dog ... but the dog first.

Ajit still seemed skeptical, so I worked overtime that week, making sure the dog gave him a lot of attention without going overboard, while also reassuring Ajit that the dog was my responsibility and not his. I would do all the feeding, walking, and handling of poop. No one else needed to get involved. I tried to give the impression that the dog would be no problem at all. When he threw up on my best dress, I didn't tell anyone. I held the puppy close and whispered, "That's all right, precious." The dog was already more important to me than the dress.

Fortunately, the dog's personality helped get us all through that first week. It didn't matter what you were busy doing—eating, reading, watching TV—he would flop down in your lap and start licking your hands. When he was tired, he was content to lie down in one place, often in the middle of the most frequently traveled path in the room. I often found myself tiptoeing around or stepping over him so that I could get where I needed to go without disturbing him. I knew who was in charge.

I also pitched to Ajit the value of owning a dog. I pointed out that dogs are probably the only creatures on earth who will give you such unconditional love. Having a bad hair day? Doesn't matter. Your dog will rush up to you, wag his tail, and demand a kiss. Feeling bad when you're down with the flu? Somehow, your dog knows, and he's right there, snuggling up next to you, providing comfort and support. "In that way, a dog is even better than chicken soup!" I said to Ajit.

Ajit already knew this but was still noncommittal. I groped around for another argument. "And he can be a guard dog," I pointed out. "A barking dog keeps out intruders, right?"

Ajit shrugged. "Wouldn't a German Shepherd be better for that?" he asked.

I hesitated. We lived part of the week in New York City and part of the week at his home in Greenwich, Connecticut. Out-of-city living was enjoyable, but people there, unlike New Yorkers, tended to worry less about crime. I couldn't get used to being alone in a big house, so a dog, I thought, would help me feel more comfortable. A Golden Retriever, a Labrador Retriever, or a German Shepherd, might have been perfect for Greenwich, where there was sizable lawn space to roam around, but how well would those large dogs fit into my Manhattan apartment? "A Cocker Spaniel seems like a great compromise," I told Ajit. "Small enough for a city apartment, big enough not to get lost in your house or yard. And I'm sure he can bark as loud as a German Shepherd."

Although having a guard dog was part of the reason for getting a puppy, it quickly became clear that my new dog wasn't well-suited to his new job. Instead of attacking or even barking at a potential intruder, he was more likely to welcome the intruder with a lick and then lead the robber to the refrigerator in hopes of getting rewarded with a treat. Naturally, I didn't mention this to Ajit.

On the last day of our trial week, Ajit decided to take the puppy out for a walk. When he returned, his cheeks were flushed, and he was smiling broadly. According to Ajit, an attractive woman had stopped him on the street and said, "Oh, look! What an adorable dog." I got the very strong sense that both Ajit and the dog had loved the attention. Maybe there are benefits to having a dog, I could sense him thinking.

That clinched the deal. In no time at all, Sona had settled in as a permanent member of my family, with frequent visits to Ajit's house in Greenwich. When he ran outside on the lawn in Greenwich, he was a brown and darting mass of fur in a sea of green. Inside the house, which was quite large, he thought he should be allowed to go anywhere he pleased. He definitely had a sense of entitlement. Finally, to make sure he didn't do too much damage to Ajit's house, we bought a protective gate and confined him to the kitchen. He was not pleased with this arrangement and sometimes whined, but I still knew he was a keeper!

Now we only needed a name for the dog. Because of his buff color, Ajit suggested the name Sona, which meant "golden" in Hindi. The only problem was that the name sounded female and not male. In the end, I decided this wasn't a big enough strike against such a unique name, and so the dog became Sona. It wasn't a surprise that Ajit, who had launched a successful career on Wall Street, chose an Indian name for the puppy. He was born and brought up in India, and while he loved America, Ajit felt a great patriotism for his homeland. He came from the powerful Nehru family dynasty, which had led the fight for India's independence from the British along with Mahatma Gandhi. His uncle, Jawaharlal Nehru, became the country's first prime minister in 1947 until his death in 1964 and his cousin, Indira Gandhi, was later prime minister for many years. For Ajit, perhaps something he loved with an Indian name was another way to connect to his past.

Besides Ajit's ancestry, I was interested in Sona's. I decided to see what I could learn about my newest family member's past. I contacted the pet store for information on Sona's breeder in Iowa and wrote to her, explaining that I had just bought one of her puppies and wanted a little background information. I described how Sona was extremely intelligent and independent, yet also very loving and highly social. On our walks, he greeted everyone, from bag ladies to schoolchildren, with the same enthusiasm.

The owner wrote back and thanked me for contacting her. As it turned out, Sona was one of three males in a litter of five. Sona's father, Rusty Boy Robinson, was a very good looking dog, the owner claimed, with an excellent disposition. He was playful and yet quasi-dignified. His mother, Penny Puddles IV, was described as quite gentle. I thought Sona probably took after his father more. I didn't ask how a dog went about getting a name like Penny Puddles IV.

The breeder went on to explain that she and her daughter ran a small kennel of about 50 dogs and that they tried to maintain as fine a grade of breeding stock as possible. While this was all probably true, Sona ended up having several medical problems during his lifetime. Eventually, I suspected that because Cocker Spaniels had been so popular at the time, there'd been a lot of inbreeding, which led to a lot of inbred dogs sold through puppy mills. Internet and retail sellers often don't check the health and the history of the dogs they're selling. Even though Sona had official papers that confirmed he was purebred, I sometimes questioned this and wondered whether he was a mixed breed. Somewhere far back in his family tree, had there been a touch of poodle? I wouldn't have minded if there had been; I loved mixed breeds. Maybe that was one reason Sona was so special. The vet always said that Sona's loving disposition was unusual for Cocker Spaniels. He wasn't snappish in that way you sometimes saw with spaniels, and he was not a complainer. Generally, he seemed to appreciate the bright side of life.

A Dozen Dog Myths

Many people, including some dog owners, are misinformed about their pets and dog behavior in general. Below are a dozen dog myths that people still tend to believe are true.

1 - Certain dog breeds are more aggressive than others.

Most people have heard the claim that pit bulls are a dangerous and aggressive breed. According to several studies, however, a dog's aggression is less attached to its specific breed and more attached to how it's brought up and treated. Without proper socialization and training, any dog can behave aggressively. The Centers for Disease Control and Prevention concluded that no dog is inherently dangerous or vicious just because of its breed.

2 - Dogs eat grass when they are sick to induce vomiting.

The reason dogs eat grass has long confounded experts, which might be a reason this myth has lingered for so long. The most current research, however, points to another reason your pet might be eating grass: An animal simply likes the taste of it, particularly when the grass is green and fresh. Unless your dog is eating grass that has been treated with harmful chemicals, there's no harm if he gets the urge to munch on the lawn from time to time.

3 - A dog is fine in a car if you've cracked open a window.

This is a dangerous myth that can put your dog at risk. Never leave your dog alone in a warm car, even if a window is cracked open and you think you'll only be gone for a couple of minutes. During warm and hot weather, the inside of a car heats up quickly, sometimes as high as 140 degrees in less than an hour. Heatstroke can be fatal to a dog in a matter of minutes. Since dogs don't sweat, it's more difficult for them to regulate body temperature and keep cool. In fact, leaving your dog alone in a car for any reason is illegal in some states. Of course, if you have a Tesla, you can simply put the car into Dog Mode. The air conditioning will go on and you don't have to worry. If the battery in your car falls to below 20 percent, you'll get an alert on your cell phone so you can go back to your pet.

4 - A dog's mouth is cleaner than a human's mouth.

While most of the germs in a dog's mouth are dog-specific and harmless to humans, this does not include where the dog's mouth and tongue have been. If your dog is tasting the concrete, drinking dirty rain water, licking its own butt, and sampling the poop of the neighbor dog or cat, those are germs that can make their way onto your face or into your mouth with one sloppy kiss from him.

5 - If a dog can run in a yard, it has no need for a walk.

While dogs may take care of business outside in the backyard, unless you are out there with them encouraging play and exercise, plan to take your dog out for a walk or a hike every day. Regular exercise helps promote stable health.

6 - Dogs are colorblind.

Color vision is possible because of specialized types of photoreceptor cells in the retina called cones. Humans have three cones, while dogs have only two. This means that although dogs can't see the full spectrum of color that a human can, they are still able to distinguish some colors. For example, a dog can tell the difference between blue and yellow but sees red and most other colors as varying shades of gray.

7 - A wagging tail is a sign of a happy dog.

Tail wagging can also indicate fear, anxiety, nervousness, and impending aggression. If a dog's tail wags slowly and erratically while inverted on a dog's back, this can be a warning sign. Tail position is also important in reading a dog's mood. If the tail is down, this usually indicates submissiveness and anxiety. A horizontal tail usually signals a calm and happy dog, while a vertical tail often signals aggression.

8 - A warm and dry nose means a dog is sick.

Chalk this one up to an old wives' tale. A dog's nose might be dry for many reasons. During sleep, it could happen because the dog isn't licking it constantly or, in cold months, because the dog is sleeping too close to a heat source. Likewise, a warm nose doesn't automatically signal a fever.

9 - You can calculate a dog's age by counting human years and multiplying by seven.

Recent research suggests this method is outdated. While aging can vary slightly in different breeds of dogs, most dogs are already teenagers (or close to it) when they're 1-year-old. The chart below gives a rough estimate of a dog's age in "human years."

Your Dog's Age	0	1	2	3	4	5	6	7	8	9	10	11	12	13	14	15	16	17	18
Age in "human years"	0	12	24	28	32	36	40	44	48	52	56	60	64	68	72	76	80	84	88

Credit: Petful.com

10 - A female dog needs to have one litter of pups before being spayed.

Unfortunately, this myth helps to foster overpopulation. There are no proven health or behavioral benefits to giving birth to a litter of pups before such a procedure. (And what happens if the mother has a dozen babies in that one litter?) There is evidence, on the other hand, that spaying reduces the risk of future health problems. For example, if it is done before the dog's first heat, her risk of getting mammary cancer later in life is reduced to almost zero.

11 - You can't teach an old dog new tricks.

This is one of the most popular and persistent myths. While it might take a little longer to train an adult dog, age is not a defining factor in its ability to learn. Since dogs learn best through motivation, find a way to motivate your dog to learn (such as with praise and a stroke on the head). Pro tip: Doggie treats are not the only way to reward a dog for learning a new trick or command. Positive reinforcement, including giving your dog a toy, or showering him with praise, should do the trick and may actually be better than food. Dogs trained with treats are often never weaned off them, and they can reach adulthood conditioned to behave as you want only if a treat is given in return.

12 - A little chocolate won't hurt.

No! Chocolate can be toxic for a dog because it contains a chemical called theobromine, which is essentially poison for your dog. According to the website Petful (www.petful.com), as little as 1 ounce of dark chocolate is enough to kill a small dog. If you feel the need to give your dog a crunchy treat, stick to biscuits that come in flavors like bacon, cheese, peanut butter, and chicken.

- 2 -

A Mind of His Own

Admittedly, I wasn't the most disciplined dog parent in Manhattan. It didn't come as a surprise to anyone who knew me that I was spoiling Sona rotten. He quickly learned all the house rules and followed them ... if he had no other choice. He was a little sneak, and Ajit and I soon started referring to him as "Mr. Opportunity." If he could pull a fast one, he would. Sona was sweet but also stubborn. If things weren't going his way, he'd let you know. He would never bite, but he'd level you with a look that said, "I'm not too pleased. Consider yourself warned."

When Sona was a puppy, he liked to sleep in my bed, often squeezing in between Ajit and me. If Ajit was traveling, Sona was even worse. He would lie next to me, content and on his best behavior. But he was also clever, and he knew how to capitalize on my affection for him. Every so often, after I'd fallen asleep, he'd give me a push, a little nudge with his nose. To make sure I didn't hurt him, I'd groggily move closer to the edge of the bed. Soon I was inches away from toppling to the floor, my arms and legs dangling over the bed, while Sona was sprawled out horizontally across the mattress.

Was he satisfied with just taking over the mattress? No, not if there was also a pillow nearby. Whenever I had to get up to go to the bathroom, he would creep up onto the pillow and stretch out. When I'd return, he was lying there like a king, looking at me as if to say, "Now, you wouldn't ask me to move from this comfortable spot, would you?" Of course, I never did. I simply sighed and, pillowless, took my spot at the edge of the bed.

I was always impressed by how Sona appreciated the finer things in life: a soft pillow, fine sheets, thick, woolly blankets. Squeaky toys were also a favorite. Often, at around 2 in the morning, I would hear the high-pitched noise of a toy, jump nearly out of my skin, and think, "Oh, God! What is that?"

Finally, I realized that if I were ever going to have another night of adequate sleep, I was going to have to make some changes. I bought Sona a wonderful bed—large, square, and wooden, raised about 11 inches off the floor, and furnished with a very comfortable down blanket and pillow. Maybe if Sona had his own bed and pillow, he wouldn't need mine? I placed the bed in the hall right next to the bedroom and left the door open, so he could see in. Sona soon adjusted to his bed and settled in. At that point, he probably had come to realize that I wasn't a sound sleeper, that I was prone to restless leg syndrome, and that his own bed meant he wouldn't have to endure any unexpected kicks.

Sona's bed antics were not the only behavior that had an opportunistic side. He also tried to get me to play with him whenever he could. I was a journalist and spent a great deal of time on the computer, writing stories and straining to meet deadlines. If Ajit and Maria were not in the apartment, and if Sona felt that I'd forgotten about him while I was typing away, he would hurry into the bathroom and grab the end of a roll of toilet paper in his mouth, and then this brown, four-legged wonder would rush from the bathroom out to the hallway, gleefully leaving a "paper trail" behind him. It was hard to miss the flash of energy as he dashed by. Then, instead of looking guilty when I stood up from my desk and tended to him, he'd look pleased and triumphant. I soon realized he didn't care what I was saying or if I was scolding him; what counted was that I was paying attention to him. Maybe he had a point about how much time I spent at my desk. When my mother was in the apartment to visit, she also took note of how much time I spent working. "Don't you think you need to get off it for a while?" she asked, essentially echoing Sona's sentiments.

Sona also loved to steal socks. He would stand in front of me with a stray sock in his mouth, holding it like a bone, and when I would start to protest, he'd dash off with a spirit of victory, hoping I would follow him. I ended up with a lot of mismatched socks this way. Sometimes I would find the socks days later, behind a chair or under the table or the sofa. If that wasn't enough, he would also take a scarf and put it right in front of him, daring me to take it away. Of course, I just hugged him. Not to be outdone, he also loved to gather up the cleaning rags whenever I was trying to make the apartment presentable. He would always take a rag to the same spot, lie down, growl, and wait for me to come and snatch it back from him. He trained me well: I soon learned to give him a treat in exchange for one of the stolen rags.

Even the newspaper wasn't safe from Sona's shenanigans. Often, he would take one from a basket of papers we kept on the floor. He would drag a few pages right in front of where I was typing at my desk, look at me with a challenging air, and then start tearing the pages up, making as much noise as possible. He would look up to make sure I was paying attention, and then shed some more paper. How could I ignore that? Eventually, I'd leave my desk, ball up some of the paper, and throw the balls around for an impromptu game of fetch. Sona would dash after the newspaper balls and bring them back to me, wagging his tail and panting. He could have done this for hours, and he seemed disappointed when I stopped after a half an hour and returned to my desk.

Other times, when I was busy at my desk and he realized that no matter what he did, or what sort of tricks he pulled, he wasn't going to get my attention, he would dash to the front window of the apartment, stand on his hind legs with his front paws on the windowsill, and gaze out at all the cars and people passing by. We lived on the fourth floor, and he loved when a fire truck or an ambulance raced past, making all that racket. He would bark with excitement, as if to say, "Hey, Mom, come see! This is so cool!" At moments like that, how could I not stop what I was doing and go over to see what Sona was up to? He was so curious and intelligent, as if he knew the sound of the fire truck was important and shouldn't be missed. Of course, someone else might say he was just plain nosey.

When Sona grew bored with spending time with me, he developed the habit of leaving my apartment, if the door was ajar, to visit neighbors. In his mind, the entire floor belonged to him, not just where we lived. His favorite neighbors, a Midwestern couple in their seventies, loved having Sona show up unannounced, so they often left their door open for him. Once inside, his favorite place in their apartment was, unsurprisingly, the refrigerator. He would head right there, looking for snacks he knew they kept. Eventually, they bought a small rug for him next to the living room sofa, and this became Sona's "spot" while they watched television and petted him. Soon Sona realized this apartment was almost as good as home—in some ways better, because at my neighbor's place, he was king and could get "handouts" in the form of doggie treats much more easily than he could with me. It got to the point that if the front door of my apartment was even slightly ajar, Sona would push the door open and dash over to my neighbor's place. Sometimes I would look up from my desk, noting the unusual silence in the apartment, and call out, "Sona, where are you? Precious, are you here?" If I received no answer and couldn't find him sleeping anywhere, I knew he'd decided another trip to the neighbors was in order.

I'll admit that there were times I should have exerted more discipline over Sona. I just couldn't help myself. Sona was always one step—or maybe several steps ahead of me. Once, he stole a loaf of bread off the kitchen table. I was awakened at 3 a.m. by a noise in the kitchen. When I hurried there, I found Sona with slices of bread sticking out of his mouth. He wouldn't let go of the bread, although he'd already eaten half the loaf and was, or so I imagined, very full.

"Please, Sona, drop it!" I pleaded, but to no avail. When I tried to snatch the bread away, he let out a small warning growl. I decided I was going to have to trick him into letting go of the bread. I found his favorite squeaky toy in the living room and brought it to the kitchen, placing the toy near him. When Sona went to pick up the toy, the bread slipped from his mouth and I snatched it up. Betrayed, Sona stared at me with disapproval. But from that experience, I learned my lesson. Bread and all other food were never left on the table again. Chairs were pushed in, so Sona couldn't jump on them and climb onto the table. I also became more aware of foods that aren't good for dogs, such as chocolate, onions, and grapes. And no sips of coffee to help perk up Sona in the mornings! All of us—Ajit, Maria, myself, and my mother when she was visiting—were on Sona patrol, making sure there was nothing harmful he could reach and get himself into trouble. This wasn't easy. Sona was always on the prowl.

Because Sona was so spoiled, he was also quite jealous. On occasion, if a friend was visiting and we were sitting on the sofa, Sona would come over, place his paws on the sofa between us, and softly growl at the intruder. The growl would start low and then scale upward as if to say, "All right, this is my house, and I'm king here." Those were instances when I probably should have taken more firm control, but I would just pick him up and place him on the sofa with us. Whatever Sona did, I had one inviolate rule: No one could hit him. No rolled-up newspapers or whacks on the behind. I enforced this rule unequivocally with my boyfriend, my assistant, my neighbors, and my friends, although none of them showed any inclination to want to lash out at Sona. We were all too under his spell.

Still, when a friend bought me a T-shirt that said, "My Dog Runs All Over Me," I got the message and pondered whether I needed help raising him. Clearly, Sona was an alpha dog who didn't listen to commands and would have full tyrannical control of the house if I didn't take charge, quickly and effectively. I noticed Sona's guarded and territorial behavior even when my mother visited me. Why couldn't he jump onto her chair if she went into the other room, and why couldn't he steal the stockings she had removed from her feet? When she was quietly eating a sandwich, why couldn't he stand under her, drooling, waiting for a morsel to fall?

Determined to show everyone I could teach Sona the difference between right and wrong, I decided to seek some help from an expert. A friend recommended Brian Kilcommons, a noted dog trainer who has a special gift with animals. On the day of our first appointment, I groomed Sona, put him on his leash and had him sitting at my side when Brian walked into the apartment. I wanted Sona to look his best and leave a good impression. But Brian took one look at Sona and me and then said, "The dog doesn't need a trainer, you do."

Brian also quickly fell in love with Sona and started to call him "pumpkin" as a pet name. "Who could forget him?" Brian said when I asked about his experiences with Sona. "Like most puppies, he didn't have any idea what he should and shouldn't be doing. You were somewhat over the moon with him. You learned how to love and give him attention, but also how to direct him. He thrived on that. It gave you a nice, happy, confident dog."

Through Brian, I learned that behavioral problems are considered somewhat common with Cocker Spaniels. "Ask some people in the industry about buff male Cocker Spaniels," Brian said, "and they'll raise their eyebrows and say 'aggression.'" But Sona, Brian said, never seemed aggressive, or hectic, frightened, or unsure of himself. "That comes from having love and consistency. And I think you respected the dog for himself. You didn't treat him like he was a little fur baby."

While genetics can play a part in the character of a pet, so does interaction between the animal and its owner. "Sometimes I look at dogs and their owners, and I think of a hostage situation," Brian told me. "The person loves the dog, but the dog is only fulfilling an emotional need. There's not an even relationship. You and Sona had a partnership, which is ideally what you want to develop between a pet and owner."

Sona and I didn't have a lot of sessions with Brian, but the ones we had were essential. I learned to listen and to understand that if I wanted Sona to take my commands seriously, I had to follow through on those commands. I asked Brian what was one of the major mistakes that pet owners make when raising and disciplining their pets. He laughed and said, "Half of the dogs in America think their name is 'No.' That's the word they hear most often. It becomes confusing and removes trust when you always have to learn through correction." He emphasized the importance of using praise and rewards to guide a dog's behavior, not just scolding. "Most people correct readily, but they won't praise very often," he said. "I think that's the way people have been taught, and so they teach their animals in the same way. Of course, you were the opposite. I had to tell you to curb back on some of the praise." He stressed that it takes time before you can expect a dog to learn all they need to know to fit into a human lifestyle. "There are no shortcuts or miracles," Brian said. "There is only understanding."

When Brian worked with Sona, I noticed that Sona behaved extremely well. It was as if Sona had gone through a few rounds at Marine boot camp, almost responding with a salute and a "Sir, yes sir!" after every command—"sit," "stay," "lie down." I marveled every time Sona made a correct and orderly move. He did everything Brian said on the first command. Brian was an experienced dog trainer who had seen every dog trick in the books and knew how to respond to it, so maybe dogs instinctively sensed that and knew, in his presence, they had to get serious. Of course, as soon as Brian was out the door, Sona would look at me with his, "Well, I'm glad that's over" expression, quickly reverting to his old self and his favorite antics. I had to learn how to make Sona respond to me with some of the same discipline he had with Brian. I taught myself how to be serious, consistent, and, most importantly, firm with Sona, so he would understand that there were limits to his behavior, even when it was just the two of us in a room together. The bottom line was to gain Sona's trust and then stay in charge.

Thankfully, Brian taught me some practical tricks that I tried to follow as often as possible. For example, he told me to fill a can with coins and tape the top shut, and when Sona did something wrong, I was to shake the can to interrupt the unwanted behavior and then teach him what I wanted him to do. This worked for a while, until Sona grew accustomed to the sound and, even if I shook the coin can until my arm ached, he just went off on his next adventure.

I learned that, when training a dog, the tone of voice is crucial. You use an enthusiastic voice to say, "Good boy!" after a dog has followed the rules. Use a middle-range voice to offer directions. A deep, low voice helps correct unwanted behavior. I spent a lot of time switching the tenor of my voice, trying to get the pitch right. Sometimes I wondered if that was one reason dogs tend to obey men more. Sona could tell the difference between the generally softer voices of women and the stronger, deeper voices of men. And he would act accordingly, which might explain why, initially, Sona was more likely to obey Ajit than he was to obey me.

Brian also told me that there were different stages in a dog's life. As a dog matures and then ages, you need to change your approach. Dealing with a puppy is different from dealing with a young dog or an older one. Fortunately for me, when Sona was between nine and 24 months old, a key period in a dog's development and a peak time for a dog to act out, he never engaged in some of the more common puppy misbehavior. There wasn't a lot of chewing on furniture or shoes, and he rarely had "accidents." He wasn't prone to jumping up on people or going into barking fits. The challenge came when Sona reached about three years old, at a point when he learned what a pushover I was and decided to capitalize on this. If I gave him a command, he would act like he hadn't heard me or move off into another room. "Sit" wasn't in his vocabulary (at least when I said it) and "don't" was ignored. For years I battled more with myself than with Sona, trying to remember what Brian had taught me about claiming control with a firm hand ... and often failing. Sona always had attitude. One of the traits that made him such a strong dog and a free spirit was also what made him feel he didn't have to play by the rules. Gradually, over the years, I came to realize that dealing with those tricks was not so much a matter of being tough as it was a matter of establishing an understanding between the two of us.

Fortunately, one thing I never had to worry about with Sona was barking. This was no small thing when you lived in an apartment building in New York City. Sona rarely barked except when excited or trying to get my attention, or when falling into his whirling dervish dance greeting. Once, there were so many barking and yapping dogs in my building that a no pet policy was adopted. Naturally, this didn't go over well with residents, including me, so the policy was quickly reversed in favor of a new one that strongly recommended that dogs not be left alone. Also, management recommended that residents hire a trainer to handle their dogs' barking. If a dog continued to bark, the owner would be fined. Even if only three or four dogs were barking in a building, the noise could become significant and even unbearable. A friend introduced me to her adorable mixed shepherd, Frankie, who would often bark at strangers and other dogs. She and her husband tried a lot of things from using dog barking control devices to simply commanding him to "stop." In the dog park, she would sit beside Frankie and say, "Good dog. Love you." She was amazed how that calmed him down.

To find out more about Brian Kilcommons, check out his books, which include *Good Owners, Great Dogs*; *My Smart Puppy: Fun, Effective, and Easy Puppy Training*; and *Childproofing Your Dog: A Complete Guide to Preparing Your Dog for the Children in Your Life*.

You can also learn more at his website, Great Dogs by Brian (www.greatdogsbybrian.com), which offers tips on training and health care, videos, as well as a weekly webinar in addition to more information on the services Kilcommons offers.

Tips for Disciplining a Puppy

According to Petcube, a small company that makes pet camera products that allow you to watch your pets on your smartphone, there are several ways owners of an exuberant puppy can discipline the new member of the family without resorting to harsh scolding and spankings.

1 - Be consistent.

You can't punish your dog for barking at the cat one day and then let the same behavior slide the next day because you're too tired or worried about seeming too strict and losing the dog's affection. A wishy-washy approach to discipline will only confuse him and likely reinforce the negative behavior. This is a tip I could never quite master when dealing with Sona.

2 - Be prompt.

Punishment is effective only if you catch a puppy in the act of misbehavior. If Fido chews up your favorite sandals and you find the chewed-up mess on the floor an hour later and scold him for it, he's not going to understand why he is being reprimanded.

3 - Be firm.

A good puppy parent understands that you need to stay in control and present an authoritative front without resorting to yelling or physical aggression. Dogs don't understand that yelling is directed at a specific behavior. They interpret the yelling as threats to themselves, which will lead to your dog fearing you and not learning what negative behavior to avoid. A firm "no" is the best way to signal to your puppy that a specific behavior is not okay.

4 - Use positive reinforcement.

Studies have shown that dogs learn more through positive reinforcement than from punishment. If Fido stops barking when you say he should stop, or he "does his business" outside instead of on grandma's homemade rug, praise him and let him know he's been a good boy or girl.

5 - Give timeouts.

Timeouts aren't just for naughty children anymore! Puppies can also learn from being put in "isolation" away from humans and other pets, usually for no longer than a couple of minutes. According to Petcube, timeouts are most effective when used in response to behaviors like pestering other dogs, nipping, or chewing.

- 3 -

A Star is Born

Finally, the time came when I thought, naively, that Sona had been sufficiently trained and had grown enough to understand right from wrong. This led me to believe he might become a star—the next Benji or Lassie—when the opportunity presented itself.

I wasn't a doggie stage mother, mind you. Sona's beauty and charisma just seemed to stand out. People noticed him. When Sona was a puppy, I was walking him down the street one day when a woman stopped to admire him. "He's so adorable!" she said. "What kind of dog is he?"

Sona had been to the groomer recently, so he didn't look like a typical Cocker Spaniel. As it turned out, the woman worked as an advertising director for a catalogue company. "Would you mind if we photograph him to appear with our model for our women's clothes catalogue?" she asked.

I was amazed and tried not to show my excitement. She handed me her card, and with a little follow-up, Sona was soon posing at his first photo shoot, which took place in front of New York City's Warwick Hotel.

The doorman stood by, watching the action in the background, as the model held Sona's leash and gazed down at him with a charmed expression. Quickly, Sona learned the first rule of being photographed: Look at the photographer! A lot of people stopped on the street to watch the photo shoot. Sona added a lot of pizzazz to the pictures, although I don't know what impact he had on sales. Still, animals, like children, have a way of stealing a shot or a scene right out from under the nose of an adult. Once I saw a very pretty model in a Talbot's catalog, and she was completely upstaged by the Cavalier King Charles Spaniel she was holding, a spaniel that I couldn't help but notice bore some resemblance to Sona.

To my surprise, Sona's appearance in the catalog did lead to better opportunities. A casting call had been put out for dogs to appear in a television commercial. When someone saw Sona's picture in the catalog, the person called the casting director, and Sona was called in for an audition. As a writer, editor, and producer myself, I clearly knew what this meant. My Sona would become a star! He even had some "experience" in front of the camera, so why not make the leap into television work?

I was so excited that, at that moment, I probably did become a stage mother. I went all out to make sure that Sona looked his best for his big breakthrough. First, I took him to his groomer, Marsha Habib, then the owner of the Sutton Dog Parlor in Manhattan, who changed his look forever. Cocker Spaniels have an almost regal look, with their silky coat and distinctive long ears that help guide scent particles towards their noses. Marsha gave Sona what we came to call his "rock star cut," curling his hair at the crown and ears. The curls offset Sona's liquid brown eyes. Most people still recognized Sona as a Cocker Spaniel, but they often asked, just to be sure.

Then I bought a new collar to top off his new and more stylish hairdo. In my eyes, Sona looked so adorable that I couldn't imagine he wouldn't get cast in the commercial.

When I arrived at the location for Sona's audition, it looked very much like a casting call. A wide variety of dogs were on display—big, small, short-hair, long-hair, purebred, and mixed. All the barking and the dogs running around, their nails clicking on the floor, made the experience exciting and even chaotic. Some of the owners were having a hard time controlling their dogs through all the commotion. Despite this, Sona remained surprisingly calm. He sat quietly beside me and took it all in. His serenity and composure amid all the canine hyperactivity convinced me that Sona would be fielding offers for TV and movie deals soon.

Finally, it was Sona's turn to audition. The director was a friendly and patient man who clearly had worked with dogs before. His assistant led Sona over to the area where he would be photographed by the cameraman. "Tell him to come," the director instructed me.

Somehow, I hadn't realized that the audition might require Sona to have to obey me. I swallowed and obeyed the director. "Sona, come!" I said, trying to indicate with my beseeching look how important it was for him to do as he was told.

Sona looked at me, yawned, and plopped down on the floor. Not for me, Sona's expression said. Other owners were dying to have their dogs cast in this commercial, and here was Sona, acting like a furry diva who was above it all!

I felt my face turn hot. "He has a mind of his own," I said and then could have bitten my tongue. Surely that wasn't something a director wanted to hear when casting a dog for a commercial. He wanted obedience and compliance, not stubborn streaks.

The director had a twinkle in his eye. "Tell him to come," he said again. This time, Sona stood up and ran in the opposite direction, then plopped down on the floor again, only farther away this time. I felt like Sona was staring right at me, and his eyes were saying, "Seriously, Mom? What are we doing here, anyway?"

The director turned to me and shrugged, a small half-smile on his face. I had the feeling he'd wanted to use Sona but realized the situation was hopeless. He probably also wondered why Sona wouldn't listen to me. "I'm sorry to have taken up your time," I apologized, feeling like a fool. I will admit that I was disappointed, and yet when I was leading Sona out of the building, all I could say was, "It's all right, Precious. I still love you!" even though my dreams of stardom for Sona had been dashed.

As for Sona, he looked indifferent to the whole fiasco. "Surely, we can do better than commercials," his expression seemed to say. Of course, it didn't matter that Sona had a great personality. With some animal acting classes, we might have had a different outcome. Sona wasn't distracted by all the action around him during the audition. He just wasn't interested. Sona was one of the lucky few chosen for potential stardom, but many dogs get a chance through animal talent agency databases. For a fee, you can submit your dog's profile. You can also check websites showing available casting calls. I was surprised to learn that Sona could have made quite a penny if he had not failed his audition. Indeed, it could have been the start of a career earning him at least $4,000 a year.

That night, after Sona's commercial experience, I was standing outside in the rain waiting for him to do his business so that I could pick up after him. I admitted to myself that while Sona might not become a TV or movie star, he was still the undisputed star of my household. I was still around to take care of all his needs.

After several minutes in the rain, Sona finally pooped. Of course, I dutifully picked up after him.

A Member of the Family

Many people don't think of their dogs just as animals, but as much-beloved members of the family. President George W. Bush once said his dog, Barney, was like the son he'd never had. Barney, at that time a three-year-old black Scottish Terrier, was the only one, or so Bush claimed, who would go fishing with him. It reminds me of a quote often attributed to President Harry Truman, "If you want a friend in Washington, get a dog." Indeed, many presidents looked to dogs for comfort and understanding.

Then there was broadcast journalist Barbara Walters, who, during an interview with Phil Donahue, talked about how much she wanted her daughter to have children because she, Barbara, was looking forward to having grandchildren. But Walters' daughter had other ideas and told her mother to get a dog instead. "And so I did!" Barbara said with a laugh.

There are more than 69 million households that own dogs, according to the American Pet Products Association. They spent $103.6 billion on their pets in 2020, and that is expected to rise to nearly $110 billion in 2021. The breakdown for 2020 expenses was as follows:

Food and treats	$42.0 billion
Supplies/Pets*/OTC Medicine	$22.1 billion
Vet Care	$31.4 billion
Pet Services	$8.10 billion

But it's not just about money. According to a 2021 survey of 2,000 cat and dog owners conducted by OnePoll on behalf of Figo Pet Insurance, a cloud-based pet health care insurance company, 81 percent wouldn't think twice before saving their pet from immediate danger and 59 percent would willingly fight another person to save their valued family member. Not surprisingly, 60 percent viewed their pet as a "soul mate." Even 84 percent of Generation Z (ages 18 to 24) would likely include pets in their wedding celebration or a milestone event, and more than 75 percent

---

* **Note:** *The APPA uses the term "live animals" instead of "pets." The $22.1 billion figure includes fish, birds, small animals, and reptiles. Pet services include grooming, training, boarding, insurance, pet sitting/walking, and all services outside of veterinary care.*

of Gen Zers might be inspired to get a tattoo resembling them as well.

Owners also looked for signs of love from their pets, as they do from their partners. Of those surveyed, 63 percent said such signs included whether their pets followed them around, while 59 percent viewed kisses from their dogs, and 53 percent believed a pet sleeping in their beds, were signs of love.

As if to confirm what dog lovers have always "known," recent studies suggest that dogs do have basic emotions, the capacity to feel joy, love, sadness, fear, disgust, anger, and curiosity. Those traits are leading owners to treat their dogs as members of the family, similar to the way they might treat their children. That applies even in the case of divorce. According to a January 2020 article at Time.com, one couple took the battle for custody of their two dogs to family court and then on to the state Supreme Court, spending about $15,000 in legal fees. They ended up splitting custody.

Some owners even take their dogs to work, which has become so popular and such a great stress reducer that the Friday after Father's Day every June is National Take Your Dog to

Work Day. Muriel Siebert, the first woman to own a seat on the New York Stock Exchange, was known to do interviews with her beloved Chihuahua, Monster Girl, at her side. When Siebert died, she left $100,000 to Monster Girl's caretaker. In her will, she wrote, "I request that my dog not be left alone for long periods of time during the day." She also donated millions for animal care and rescue. A friend of mine, Paula Dinkins, also didn't want to leave her dog alone and took her everywhere, even to Gracie Mansion when her father-in-law, David Dinkins, was the mayor of New York City.

I still remember a story some years ago about a couple from South Africa who were on a three-month sailing trip to Madagascar when their yacht, The Boundless, hit a reef near East London and they started to sink. The man, Graham Anley, sent out a radio distress call and activated their emergency position indication radio beacon, but he and his wife, Cheryl, realized they were going to have to abandon ship. Graham promptly grabbed his nine-year-old Jack Russell Terrier, Rosie, and swam safely to shore. Then he went back to assist Cheryl, whose safety line had become snagged on the steering gear. The joke became that their marriage might not be so "rosie" after that, and this was one husband whose wife was likely to banish him to the doghouse for some time.

- 4 -

It Takes an Urban Village

No matter how much I loved Sona and believed I could offer him everything he needed, I still had to devote a lot of time to my busy lifestyle as a journalist. I wrote articles for magazines as diverse as *Parade, McCall's, Reader's Digest,* and *AARP: The Magazine.* I also did interviews for the book *My Soul Looks Back in Wonder: Voices of the Civil Rights Experience.*

Sometimes my journalistic work required that I fly off on assignment. Once I was assigned by *Parade Magazine* to interview Sheila Widnall, our country's first female secretary of the Air Force. This required me to fly to Washington to meet her, spend time parachute-training, and finally suit up and fly on a B-52 bomber with her to Barksdale Air Force Base in Northwest Louisiana, where she inspected our country's missiles. Obviously, I couldn't cart Sona along with me on a B-52 bomber—even if he was a daring puppy. It was only when I returned to Washington with the secretary that we learned that her staff, lined up on the tarmac to salute her return, had actually taken bets on whether I would need a barf bag. "Who, me?" I smiled.

By this time, I'd broken up with Ajit. I thought I would marry him, and so did his family, who had welcomed me to India and their home. In the end, I realized we would be better as friends. Ajit always retained visitation rights to Sona, who long ago had worked his magic on him. Fortunately, Maria was still working with me, but she had her own schedule to keep and couldn't always dog-sit for Sona while I was away.

Enter my friends Martha and John Gallagher, who had become like a second set of parents to Sona. The first day Martha saw Sona, their bond was immediate. Sona, still a puppy then, was at the open front door of my apartment when the building elevator stopped on our floor and Martha stepped out. Sona dashed out of the apartment, tail wagging, to greet her. "Hello, wee one," Martha said in her alluring Irish accent. Sona reciprocated the greeting by licking her hands.

From that moment on, both were smitten.

Within a month, Sona had become a regular visitor to her home in Queens Village, totally settling in. Martha and John had a natural connection with Sona. Perhaps there was something to the adage that the Irish have a way with dogs! When we decided it was time for Sona to visit, I would pay for a car service to take him to Queens. Martha would ride to Manhattan in the car, we would load Sona into the back seat with her, surrounded by his toys and favorite blanket, and off he'd go. There came a point where the car service drivers even recognized Sona.

In fact, John was the one who housebroke Sona. When Sona first went to visit the Gallaghers, he was still "doing his business" pretty much whenever and wherever he pleased. "I came home one day from Mass and there were four turds on the floor," John told me once. "I cleaned them up, of course, and then fed him. When he was about to make another poop, I caught him just in time, took him out to the yard, and he made it there." Once they came back inside, John kept a watchful eye on him. When Sona had to go to the bathroom again, John took him back outside. "Well, that did it," John said. "No more inside poops. If he wanted to go outside, he'd walk to the door and stand there until I'd let him out."

I wasn't sure how John's house training had yielded such quick results when mine hadn't, but I didn't question it. Irish to the core, the Gallaghers soon started calling Sona "the wee one." It wasn't unusual at times for John to speak to Sona in Irish, and Sona often acted as if he understood.

Because Sona was so smart, it didn't take long for him to figure out that life with Martha and John was a lot more fun than with just me. He got more variety and pampering that way. The Gallaghers and I soon settled into a pattern where Sona generally spent two weeks with me in my Manhattan apartment and two weeks with them at their home in Queens. He always got the "zoomies" when he came home, showing his happiness by wagging his tail and running around in circles. But I couldn't help wonder if he wished he could have stayed at the Gallaghers' place a little longer.

And who could blame him if he had wanted to? They lived in a lovely area with plenty of trees, sunshine, blue sky, friendly neighbors, and a backyard in which Sona could chase squirrels. None of that chaotic city life he had with me—crowded streets, honking cars, traffic congestion, pesky tourists, and dogs with attitude. At the Gallaghers' place, he was pampered with the finer things in life. When John cooked oatmeal in the morning, he always gave a portion to Sona, not to mention a little tea and toast during the midday break.

Unfortunately, Sona developed some undesirable traits from all this lavish attention. For one, he became even more territorial. If you were sitting in what he thought of as "his" chair and he wanted you to move, he would stare until you grew uncomfortable or felt guilty and took the hint. And he also, for a dog so adorable, occasionally exhibited a bad temper. If he didn't want you to do something, or if you were acting in a way that didn't meet his approval, he would make his displeasure clear. His favorite way to communicate disapproval was to sit on his haunches and not move. No amount of cajoling or sweet talk could get him to budge. And while he adored being petted, he did not like people stroking or scratching his ears too much. When someone tried, he'd pull his head back, and the expression on his face said, "You'd better be careful, there." In short, despite Brian Kilcommons' careful training, there were a few times when Sona could be intimidating. Negotiation was not in his vocabulary. Instead, he would growl and tug on the leash until I yielded and let him stay out for a bit longer. While some people might have seen this behavior as Sona believing that he was running the show, I reminded myself that Sona was still a puppy, and like a child, could be stubborn when testing his independence.

From the time he was a puppy, Sona always hated taking baths. He couldn't stand water of any temperature or the feel of waterlogged hair. If he was at Martha and John's place and heard Martha saying, "I think we'd better bathe Sona. He smells," he would hide out for the rest of the day, primarily under their kitchen table. No amount of coaxing could convince him to come out, and his hardy resistance often made John and Martha rethink the bath.

While Sona was cute and in general good with people, he was also very wily. Martha tried hard to set Sona on the right path, but John was often an unwitting ally to

Sona's misbehavior. If Sona misbehaved, such as chewing on the leather strap of Martha's watch, Martha would scold him, "Sona, no! That's bad, Sona!" Affronted, Sona would stop chewing long enough to turn to John and cast him a disdainful look, as if to say, "Aren't you going to tell that wife of yours she can't say no to me?" As hard as John tried backing Martha up by saying, "She's right, Sona, you can't do that," his tone was so soft, so unauthoritative that Sona heard, "Go ahead, Sona. Enjoy yourself. Don't pay her any mind." And Sona would go right back to chewing on the leather strap of her watch.

If John started scolding Sona for any reason, Sona would chase him up the stairs, playfully nipping at his heels. At other times, Sona would run halfway up the stairs, then turn around and growl. Then he'd dash away to find Martha and search for sympathy there. Clearly, John wasn't the boss as far as Sona was concerned. He would listen to Martha when he had to, but reluctantly.

Despite these occasional personality clashes, John and Martha deeply enriched the quality of Sona's life. Maria had also developed a lasting relationship with Sona, who trusted her completely. She was available to walk, feed, and play with him, a devoted companion who was always there for him when the Gallaghers or I couldn't be. And Maria was the only one who Sona allowed to bathe him, and that included me!

Sometimes, when I was away for business or pleasure, Maria took Sona to her home in a third-floor walk-up apartment in Queens. Her building didn't have an elevator, and although Sona weighed about 30 pounds, Maria would carry him up and down the stairs to her apartment. No wonder Sona grew so fond of her. She was his own personal elevator! And Sona, being Sona, acted as if getting carried up and down three flights of stairs was the most natural thing in the world.

Home Away from Home

What should dog owners do if they don't have a Maria, John, or Martha in their lives to help share the responsibilities of caring for a dog? Fortunately, in this era of internet access and a booming pet care service industry, there are a variety of options for people who need help in caring for their pets.

If you're leaving town, diligent research and expert referrals are instrumental in finding a good kennel for your dog. Make sure you visit the kennel beforehand, so you can view the accommodations and get a sense of the owners and the other dogs they house there. Ask about the play, feeding, and exercise schedules. Do not assume that all kennels are created equal! If you have the time, it's a good idea to comparison shop so that you can find the right kennel for your needs. Check that the facility conforms to minimum kennel standards: The area is clean, well-lit, and well-ventilated; there's adequate space for dogs to play; dogs have consistent access to water and shelter; the kennel practices environmentally sound waste management procedures. Ask whether all the dogs in the facility are current on their vaccinations, because kennels that house unvaccinated dogs can become a breeding ground for communicable diseases such as Bordetella. Finally, some kennels might offer special "boutique" services, like allowing owners who are away from their dog to spend quality time with their pets on Skype or FaceTime.

If you prefer a more personal approach, such as hiring a sitter to stay with your dog at your home, ask family, friends, and neighbors for recommendations.

You can also find useful information at Care.com (www.care.com) Sittercity (www. sittercity.com) or Rover (www.rover.com)

Make sure that anyone you hire to take care of your pet understands the specific needs of your dog. Write down a list of particulars—what food they like or don't like—for whomever will be caring for your pet, since many animals can be finicky. Don't forget to give the caretaker the phone numbers and addresses of both your regular and emergency veterinarians. Many emergency veterinary hospitals around the country are open late at night, and some are even open 24 hours a day. Like the emergency room at a hospital, they offer immediate urgent care and can be a lifesaver for an animal in serious trouble.

Finally, inform the dog sitter about any health conditions your dog might have. There was a case where a man was hired to dog-sit for a woman's Labradoodle for a week. The dog was prone to epileptic seizures, but the owner did not inform the dog sitter of this. Understandably, the dog sitter was alarmed when the dog started drooling and stumbling around the room, and then collapsed in a heap on the floor.

Taking Fido on the Road

If you want to take your pet with you, there are countless hotels worldwide that are pet friendly.

PetSmart Pet Hotels, for example (services.petsmart.com/petshotel) offers doggie day camps where your dog can play, exercise, and socialize with other dogs, as well as overnight boarding (if you're willing to pay the price) and even private suites for dogs who appreciate more lush accommodations and private pampering.

Other sites, including Travelocity (www.travelocity.com), Petswelcome (www.petswelcome.com), BringFido (www.BringFido.com) and TripsWithPets (www.tripswithpets.com) also provide lists of pet-friendly hotels in the U.S. and abroad. You can also go to the American Kennel Club (www.akc.org) for its guide to dog-friendly hotel chains in the U.S. Or consult the websites of hotels you are considering staying in. Most pet-friendly hotels are in the lower-priced to mid-priced range, but there are also hotels for those who are able and willing to pay for more luxurious accommodations.

The Kimpton Muse Hotel in New York City, for example (www.themusehotel.com) long provided dogs with a welcome amenity such as a toy, a collar tag, or treats, as well as a water bowl, a squeaky toy, a pooper scooper, a leash, and a special door sign - "Do Not Disturb" - style that let staff members know a pet was in the room. Last but not least, it included a copy of *The New York Paws*, a guide to area parks, shops, pet sitters, and animal hospitals. Due to the Covid-19 pandemic, the Kimpton Muse isn't currently offering these services, though it expects to bring them back in the future. For now, Fido will have to settle for a blue Frisbee with the Muse logo on it when he arrives at the front desk.

- 5 -

The Animal Medical Center

While Sona appeared to be a healthy and energetic puppy, he faced a series of medical challenges over his 15 years of life. Fortunately, the world's largest nonprofit animal hospital is in New York City: The Animal Medical Center focuses on advanced veterinary treatment, research, and education for dogs, cats, and exotic animals. For Sona and me, it would become another home, not to mention a vital source on the latest information and recommendations for keeping Sona healthy.

Open 24 hours a day, the Animal Medical Center employs more than 100 veterinarians with expertise in more than 20 specialties. It also offers a very helpful Pet Health Library (www.amcny.org/pet-health-library) that will assist you in knowing when it's time to consult a veterinarian. The AMC website (www.amcny.org) also gives updates on current clinical trials and provides information on whether your pet is eligible to participate. While it's not always possible to get into a clinical trial, the owners of pets that do qualify find that the trials offer a ray of hope.

Any time I needed to take in Sona for one reason or another, I was always fascinated by the variety of animals at the center for treatment, including rabbits, parrots, and snakes, not to mention dogs representing every breed and cross-breed combination you could imagine, along with cats who always seemed a little more independent than dogs. The doctors at the clinic were gentle and mindful, not only to their animal patients but also to the owners, the animal "parents" who were worried about their pets' health. I was often reminded how common it is for pet owners to view their pets as children. I noticed this tendency from owners representing all strata of society, from the very wealthy to those struggling to pay their electric bills. It reminded me of when I once volunteered at a New York City pet clinic aimed at owners who are homeless or lack financial resources. Although they had so little, they cared for their animals with such devotion and attentiveness. In many cases, their pets were the only friends they had, offering them protection, a feeling of worth, a routine to their lives, and even a sense of purpose.

Everyone tells me I'm a worrier, and I guess it's true. I would always imagine the worst happening with Sona at the Animal Medical Center, trying to put on a brave front. But my heart kept sinking as time went by while Sona was with the vet. You can imagine my enormous relief when Sona was returned to my arms looking much better, but not quite up for a lick and a kiss, with a knowing smile from the vet and a prescription for some medicine. The vet would say, "He'll be just fine." I was always so grateful to hear those words.

The Animal Medical Center has its own pharmacy, so it was very easy to follow through on their instructions promptly. Not that Sona was always pain-free. Several times he had to wear the "cone of shame" so that he wouldn't chew his stitches or scratch at the area in which he'd been operated. Sona was not pleased whenever he had to return home with that plastic cone around his head, which was also uncomfortable. Sona's general nature occasionally made him a tricky patient to "read," according to Gene Solomon, DVM, who was Sona's vet throughout his life. "He was always such a good dog and very stoic," Dr. Solomon said. "You could never tell when he was in pain because he wouldn't whimper or cry at every touch."

Some of the health problems Sona faced over the years included pancreatitis, which occurred when he was several years old and stole a large piece of ham. In general, high-fat food is not good for a dog. While Sona didn't normally eat a high-fat diet, the ham was enough of a shock to his system that he quickly became ill. When he vomited repeatedly and then was also hit with a case of diarrhea, I was panicked. After a three-day stay with Dr. Solomon, he came home and made a full recovery. That experience didn't cure him of wanting to steal food, but it cured me of making it easy for him. I became more careful about putting away food and not leaving it unattended.

Beware of Marijuana and Your Dog

Today, with the legalization of marijuana across the country, Dr. Solomon says dog owners need to be diligent about more than just food. More dogs than ever now come into his practice suffering from the toxic effects of cannabis. "People often tell me, 'my dog got into my stash and ate my gummies!'" Dr. Solomon warns that within 40 minutes of picking up a discarded butt or consuming an edible THC—the active, psychogenic ingredient in marijuana—can become toxic, affecting the dog's gastrointestinal tract and causing him to vomit or even dribble urine. THC can also affect a dog neurologically, with him becoming unusually quiet or unsteady on his feet. Your dog may also seem more sensitive than usual to touch and sound. How long the symptoms last depends on how much was ingested. If this happens to your dog, Dr. Solomon advises that you get to the vet as quickly as possible.

During Sona's lifetime, he also suffered from several diseases and conditions, including arthritis, liver disease, heart disease, and kidney problems. Early on, he had trouble with his eyes, which only got worse as he got older. And while that list of health issues felt occasionally daunting, I still considered us lucky that Sona didn't suffer from the two "biggies" for dogs: cancer, the No. 1 killer of older dogs, and diabetes. Nor did he have canine cognitive dysfunction, sometimes called "canine senility," "canine dementia," or "dogzheimers," which produces similar symptoms in dogs as in humans:

- Sleep-wake cycle disturbances
- Generalized anxiety
- Disorientation (such as getting lost inside the house)
- Decreased activity
- Inappropriate barking and whining
- Repetitive behaviors (pacing, circling, spinning)

Sona's heart problems brought us into direct contact with Philip Fox, DVM, a nationally known expert in veterinary cardiology at the Animal Medical Center. Dr. Fox told me that Sona suffered from cardiomyopathy, which weakens and enlarges the heart muscle, making it harder for the heart to pump blood and circulate it to the rest of the body. This serious and chronic condition can lead to congestive heart disease. Needless to say, my heart sank as I listened to him. Although there is no cure, it can be treated and it's fair to say that Dr. Fox pulled Sona and me through some very serious touch-and-go moments for a long time. He always kept me calm and optimistic that Sona would make it through each crisis. It was clear that Dr. Fox cared deeply for his animal patients, establishing a bond with them and an understanding of what their owners were going through.

If you're interested in helping the Animal Medical Center continue its great work, the AMC website lists ways you can offer support: (www.amcny.org/more-ways-to-support-amc).* As with all charitable organizations, general cash donations are also always welcome. Gifts can be made online, or you can mail them to:

Animal Medical Center
Attn: Development Office
510 East 62nd Street
New York, NY 10065

---

* **Note:** *The Animal Medical Center has 12 charitable funds to help pets in need. In 2020, the AMC donated $4.8 million in veterinary care through these charitable funds. A complete listing and a description of each fund can be found on the AMC's website (www amcny.org/community-funds).*

Dog and Human Disease Connection

According to a 2017 article published by researchers at the University of California, Davis, dogs have greater than an 80 percent genetic similarity to humans, versus only 67 percent for mice. Today there are medical therapies and tests developed for humans, such as MRIs, organ transplants, dialysis, and sophisticated treatments for cancer, that can be used for dogs, including prescribing the anti-nausea drug Cerenia, which can help relieve motion sickness in dogs as well, as help manage the side effects of chemotherapy treatment in humans.

While it's far less common that advances in veterinary medicine help humans, animals have long been used in research to find solutions to diseases afflicting humans. It was fascinating to learn, for example, that Adam Mamelak, MD, a neurosurgeon at Cedars-Sinai Medical Center in Los Angeles, has performed operations to remove brain tumors from the pituitary glands of both dogs and humans in the fight against Cushing's disease, which every year affects only a few hundred people, but about 100,000 dogs.

One exciting development is being tested on dogs that could hold promise for people with glioblastoma, the same deadly cancer that killed Senator John McCain and President Joe Biden's son, Beau. The National Institutes of Health is funding a $3.4 million study conducted by Mount Sinai Health System in conjunction with Johns Hopkins University that is focused on dogs that have spontaneously developed glioblastoma tumors. The results could eventually lead to therapies for humans. Here are some others:

1 - Short-legged dogs share a gene similar to the one that causes dwarfism in humans.

Dachshunds, French Bulldogs, Pekingese, and other short-legged dogs are more likely to suffer from back pain and limb paralysis. Researchers discovered a genetic mutation that causes both a dog's short legs and, intervertebral disc disease, a mutation that resembles the one that leads to dwarfism in humans. Hopefully, methods discovered to help dogs with intervertebral disc disease might also lead to new methods of treatment for degenerative disc disease in humans.

2 - Some brain tumors can be common to dogs and people.

Certain dog breeds, such as Boxers, Bulldogs, and Boston Terriers, are more likely to develop a specific brain tumor known as a glioma, which causes a decline in brain function. Researchers discovered that the glioma develops from cell to tumor in similar ways in both humans and dogs. Since the spontaneous gliomas are the most common form of malignant brain tumors in humans and occur at a similar frequency in dogs, researchers are hopeful that they can find a link in the treatment of glioma tumors in both humans and dogs.

3 - Veterinarians test immune therapy in clinical trial.

Because dogs are prone to the same carcinogenic environmental factors as humans and can get cancer as spontaneously as humans, researchers are using an immune therapy that shrinks lung cancer in dog patients. They are also experimenting with using a dog's natural immune cells, which reject infections, to attack osteosarcoma, a bone cancer similarly found in adults.

4 - Cleft palate research for humans grows, thanks to canine study.

You've probably seen many pictures of children with cleft palates circulating around the internet. Some dogs suffer from the same condition. Cleft palate, a facial malfunction that splits open the upper lip, affects 1 in every 1,500 babies annually. Now, researchers have identified the genetic mutation that causes cleft palate in dogs and have also discovered that dogs who suffer from the condition tend to have shortened lower jaws that resemble humans who have a form of cleft palate known as Pierre Robin sequence.

The Rising Cost of Pet Health Care

The cost of health care is increasing not only for humans but also for pets. Medical and technological advances have led to longer life expectancies for dogs. As a result, health care costs are rising as dogs encounter old age health issues such as arthritis, dementia, and heart disease, according to the American Pet Products Association.

What's behind this trend? One reason is that more people are viewing their pets as family members (see Chapter 3). For previous generations of pet owners, if a pet received a life-threatening diagnosis, the next step was either immediate euthanasia or a predetermined amount of money the pet owners were willing to spend. There's even a name for it: "stop treatment point." The more a pet is viewed as a valued family member, the more money owners are willing to spend on their health care. After all, you wouldn't place a stop treatment point on the life of your child, or spouse, or parents, or Auntie Flo, would you?

While some pet owners can afford tens of thousands of dollars in medical bills, for the rest of us, a bill that large could lead to financial hardship. The solution may lie in how we handle human medical costs: insurance. There are many health insurance plans for pets that make sense from a financial standpoint, yet only 2.6 million dogs were insured in 2020, according to the North American Pet Health Insurance Association. As health care costs continue to skyrocket, many experts predict that more pet owners will sign up for insurance.

- 6 -

"Age Is Not a Disease"

Many people assume that when a dog has reached "a certain age," its life is over. Eveline Han, VMD, formerly a gastroenterologist in small-animal medicine at the Animal Medical Center, disagrees with this assessment. "Age is not a disease," she told me. For both humans and dogs, age is a state of mind. Often, it's not how old a dog is, but how well cared for and how well he's treated that can determine not only his quality of life but also the length of it. Dr. Han, who treated Sona during the last year of his life, once mentioned how impressed she was that Sona, despite his many health problems, many of which could have shortened his life, just kept on fighting. "He definitely had a will to live, and that's so important," she told me.

It's true that Sona showed a lot of courage and pluck in the face of adversity, and his positive spirit and attitude truly inspired and strengthened me. As is the case with many dogs, as Sona grew older he faced increasingly difficult and complicated health problems. Caring for an aging dog in that condition can be costly and time-consuming, requiring a good deal of patience and fortitude. What can make a big difference is the support and assistance of a top-notch, supportive, and highly qualified veterinarian. Fortunately, Sona and I had Dr. Solomon as his devoted primary vet. Dr. Solomon did his internship at the Animal Medical Center and then went on with a fellow graduate to form the Center for Veterinary Care, a very successful practice in New York City, where he treats dogs of the famous and not so famous.

I'll never forget the first time I took Sona to his office, and neither will Dr. Solomon. "He was the cutest little puppy," he told me. "We had an immediate bond. He was such a sweetheart! Even though I'd only just met Sona, and I was poking and prodding him, I noticed that Sona was very tuned in to me and what was going on around him. He really listened and wasn't rambunctious." Dr. Solomon added that he was impressed that he was able to do anything he needed to do, from examining his ears, teeth, and nails, to taking blood and performing the total exam. "He was an ideal patient," Dr. Solomon said. "Some puppies are a little bit flighty. They're busier."

Having given Sona rave reviews, Dr. Solomon's first recollection of me wasn't quite so positive. He described me as "a nervous mom," although he was quick to add that nervous moms can also make the best ones, because when anything is out of the ordinary, they notice the discrepancy and are attentive to remedying the situation. "Sona always got the best care because you knew every step, every lick, everything he did was either normal or not normal, and that was what you followed up on," Dr. Solomon said. "You didn't miss a trick. All his ailments and problems—as soon as they happened, you were on top of them. I'm sure this contributed to his quality of life."

Occasionally, Dr. Solomon made old-fashioned house calls, coming to my apartment to see Sona when he was too sick to be taken into the office. I knew this was unusual and realized what an exceptional and caring vet he was. Dr. Solomon mentioned that one likely cause of Sona's many ailments was inbreeding. He was surprised I'd bought Sona at a pet store. "If you are going to get a purebred, go to a breeder with an established reputation," he said. Now, with the internet at our fingertips, gathering information about breeders is relatively easy. If there are any unsatisfactory or even crooked breeders out there, someone will eventually expose them with an online review.

Dr. Solomon also had important advice about how to find a vet that's right for your dog. "It depends on compassion," he said. "Obviously, knowledge and the ability to recognize symptoms, and being a good doctor are critical. But what also comes into account is compassion, concern, love for animals, and personality. Basically, it's the same thing you would look for in your own doctor." Dr. Solomon recommended that the owner meet with the vet and observe the vet's interaction with the pet. "How the pet reacts to the veterinarian is crucial," he said. "There's no exact formula. It's just a gut feeling."

Additional Tips for Finding the Right Vet

If you're interested in more advice about how to find the right vet for your dog, the website PetMD (www.petmd.com) provides tips. Also consider the following.

1 - Ask around.

Use your own personal network of family, friends, neighbors, and even local shelters to seek recommendations. Good word of mouth will point you in the right direction.

2 - Choose friendly.

As Dr. Solomon suggested, a vet's credentials will only get you so far. You'll also want to consider more personal characteristics. Is the staff friendly when you call? Are they warm and engaging when you visit? Do they pay attention, or do they seem like they're trying to hurry you along? A good vet makes a client feel soothed, not stressed out.

3 - Connect on pet-care philosophies.

Make sure you see eye to eye with a prospective vet on difficult situations such as euthanasia, cancer care, and neutering and spaying. If you don't get a sense that the vet cares as much about the quality of life of your pet as you do, look elsewhere.

4 - Busier usually equals better.

Sometimes we prefer to go to quiet, uncrowded offices. But is this necessarily the best measure when searching for a good veterinary office? If you arrive at an office that is standing room only and overflowing with pets waiting to see the doctor, this could indicate that the vet is popular and trusted by many pet owners.

5 - Money matters.

Veterinary bills have always been hefty and are climbing higher every year (see Chapter 5). Before deciding on a vet, ask about the cost of routine vaccines and X-rays, how they expect payment, and whether they offer a credit line.

6 - Hours of operation.

Most people want a vet located near their homes, which is understandable. But don't forget other, equally important considerations. What hours is the office open? How do they handle an emergency patient? What are their after-hours policies? It doesn't help to have a vet near your home if the office isn't open when you need assistance.

7 - Get a second opinion.

People often seek second opinions from doctors about their own health matters, so why should you do any differently where your pet's health is concerned? A serious diagnosis or surgery for your pet is troubling for a pet owner, and a good vet will understand and not get offended if you request a second opinion. You can also ask a prospective vet if they use a referral clinic.

Ajit Hutheesing and I were proud parents of Sona, spoiling him rotten, although it took Ajit longer to succumb to his charms.

Ajit and I went to India to meet his family, including Rajiv Gandhi, prime minister of India, and his wife, Sonia. They were also dog lovers.

My mother Nora Pierce, called "Nan" by everyone, visited from her home in New Orleans, Louisiana. She was guarded when she met Sona, but was soon smitten.

Sona was lucky to have Dr. Gene Solomon as his vet. It was love at first sight. He was, Dr. Solomon said, "the perfect patient."

PONCHITTA PIERCE

GOOD MORNING DOC!

I hear you've gone Hollywood on me -- and will be out with the stars all month. What a life!

Well as you can see, I returned from Camp Gallagher (after three weeks) full of love, good food and just a little bit sassy.

But I couldn't wait to see you, for the usual:

              BUTT

              EYES

              EARS

*SHOT -- I haven't had an allergy shot in at least a month. I seem to be doing fine. Do I need to get a shot for a while?

            WEIGHT (don't forget my long
                   hair also makes me look fat)

            BACK RIGHT LEG (I seem to limp a
            little -- do you think it's all
            right?

Mom is a little crazy today. She is doing a TV show tonight. BUT, she wants you to call her in the morning -- if possible -- she has new developments for the dog show and wants to touch base before you go back to California.

AND -- how are you. Still dating wonderful ladies and all!

LICKS AND KISSES — Sona

1/15/91

It was unique for a dog, but Sona would write to Dr. Solomon to say what was wrong with him. Of course, he did have some help.

I knew Sona would continually outwit me if I didn't get the upper hand. The answer was dog expert Brian Kilcommons, who trained Sona... and me.

At first, Maria Nikolakopoulos wasn't a dog person, but she and Sona soon came to adore each other. Their special bond lasted his entire life.

As he started getting older, it was easier on Sona to bathe him in the kitchen sink. He loved to have Maria do it. "Mi amor," she called him.

Michael Werboff was an internationally known and gifted Russian painter. I was surprised and honored when he asked if he could paint my portrait.

Sona loved to play and be in the spotlight. His favorite tricks included stealing socks, often hiding them where they couldn't be found.

When socks weren't good enough, he would lie in front of one of my favorite scarves, as if to say, "Did you see this?"

I was amazed and excited when I was asked if Sona could be photographed for a Talbots catalog. Sona just took it in his stride.

- 7 -

Keeping Your Dog Fit and Trim

Any vet will tell you that major factors in how well your dog ages are your pet's diet, exercise regime, and quality of life. This doesn't mean that the dog's gene pool or the specific health problems of certain breeds are not important. Golden Retrievers, for example, are prone to hip dysplasia and cancer, as well as cardio and respiratory problems, but nutrition and exercise are areas where an owner has a fair amount of control over his dog's health.

Forget about leaving food decisions to your dog! Most dogs, if they have their way, will eat as much as they can and whatever they can, no matter how bad it is for them. Unfortunately, many owners equate letting their dog eat whatever it wants with how much they love their pet. They're a sucker for the sad-eyed pup who stares as you open a cheese wrapper or pull a piece of chicken off a bone. Beware of well-meaning but unhelpful interference from your friends, too.

A survey released by the Association for Pet Obesity Prevention (APOP) in 2019 found that 56 percent of dogs and 60 percent of cats are classified as clinically overweight or obese by their vets. Those percentages translate into 50.2 million dogs and 56.5 million cats that are too heavy.

Obviously, animals are being overfed by their owners. Some estimates suggest that a worrying 90 percent of dog owners don't know how many calories their dog should have and are prone to handing out treats whenever the dog starts begging. A survey by the company Hill's Pet Nutrition, done with the strategic consulting agency Kelton Global, showed that the situation got worse during the Covid-19 pandemic as owners fed their pets more. Interesting that 2 in 3 vets say 64 percent of pet owners were either surprised or defensive when confronted with their pet's weight issues.

A dear friend of mine, Michael Werboff, a world-famous and gifted Russian painter, loved to sneak a treat to Sona whenever he visited. Misha, as he was called, had decided to paint a portrait of me. About every three weeks he would come over for breakfast to discuss his work. As soon as Misha sat down at the table, Sona would rush over and position himself at his side. Each time Misha took a bite of his meal, he slipped a morsel to Sona. The two of them had their act down to a science and seemed to believe I was totally unaware of their collusion. There was no point in saying, "No, Misha, you can't do that. Sona should not have toast with butter and jam, eggs, or bacon." He would just look directly at me and continue to speak while slyly moving his hand toward Sona's mouth. And if I couldn't train Misha to stop with the illicit feedings, there was no hope I could get Sona to stop with the illicit eating.

As he got older, Sona's appetite increased rather than decreased. There was never a food Sona didn't like. When we went on walks, he always had his head down, hoping to find some delicious treat abandoned on the street—a pizza crust, a slice of bagel, chicken bones. If he came across any tidbit, he was as swift as a Hoover vacuum sucking up the food into his mouth. Since Sona would eat anything, anytime, anywhere, it was up to me to make sure he didn't become too fat. By the time he was five, I had to switch to an Iams dog food designed for less active dogs, to keep his weight under control. Fortunately, he loved vegetables, which helped. Each day he dined on carrots and broccoli, primarily because I ate them as well. "Anything good enough for you is good enough for me," seemed to be Sona's motto.

I always remember what one doctor told me about dogs in the wild versus domesticated animals. "Dogs today eat a lot more than they should, and they don't have the same natural environmental conditions that wild animals do, chasing after other animals," she said. "They don't have to go out and catch the next meal. The next bowl of food is right there in front of them. They lead a very sedentary lifestyle." Keeping that in mind, remember the basics of diet: Always measure pet food, and lay off the salty snacks.

One positive thing about Sona's voracious appetite was that I was able to use it to my advantage when giving him his medicine, particularly in his later years, when he had to take so many pills, which, like most dogs, he didn't like doing. Because he was so intelligent, he quickly learned to hide the pills in his mouth and dispose of them later, when no one was watching. Often, I found the rejected pills in neat little piles all over the apartment.

Not to be outsmarted, I decided to trick Sona into taking his medications. I started trying to hide his pills in cottage cheese, Parmesan cheese, Gerber's baby food (chicken and turkey flavors were his favorites.) Finally, I came upon a winning formula: I wrapped Sona's pills in fresh, 100 percent whole-wheat Wonder Bread, and then wrapped it with oven-roasted Butterball turkey slices. Sona loved these culinary treats so much he gobbled them up ... along with the medications.

Another area of a dog's well-being that owners tend to overlook is teeth. According to VCA Animal Hospitals, more than 80 percent of dogs over the age of three have active dental disease. This probably shouldn't come as a surprise since people often neglect their own dental needs. Most pet owners are a little cowardly when it comes to brushing their dogs' teeth. I certainly was.

For Sona, who did not like anyone fooling around with his mouth, we dealt with the issue by scheduling yearly dental cleanings. He would go to the vet in the morning, and while there, he would receive anesthesia and have his teeth thoroughly cleaned. When he developed heart problems, we were in a bind: General anesthesia can dangerously lower a dog's heart rate, but bad teeth can lead to bacterial infection that can have a negative impact on the heart. I tried to have his teeth cleaned by his vet for as long as it was possible. After that we prayed no infections would develop.

John de Jong, DVM, former president of American Veterinary Medical Association, pointed out in a weekly column that he writes for the *Boston Herald* that if your dog has trouble chewing hard food and has bad breath, you're already in trouble. The bad breath, which some pet owners describe as smelling like garbage, can arise from periodontal disease, tooth decay, or general dental neglect. Dr. de Jong says that symptoms of bad oral hygiene in your dog include plaque buildup, loose teeth, bleeding from the mouth, excessive drooling, and habitual pawing at the side of the face. Remember, also, that a dog's dental care is crucial at any age.

I always wished I had gotten Sona used to daily teeth brushing when he was a puppy, which would have made things less complicated in his later years. And no, you shouldn't use your family toothpaste for your dog. Of course, people don't swallow toothpaste, but dogs may, and the ingredients can upset their stomachs or worse. Xylitol, for example, which is found in regular toothpaste and is considered unharmful to humans, can be toxic to dogs, causing hypoglycemia within 10 to 15 minutes of ingestion. Fortunately, there are special canine toothpastes available at most pet supply stores. For the more inventively minded, you can make your own with baking soda and water. And for a simple solution, dry dog food can help with your dog's oral health. The grinding action while your dog is chewing helps clean the surface of the teeth, where bacteria and plaque can build up.

I also had to make sure Sona got enough exercise to stay in good health. When he was young and energetic, I could hardly keep up with him, but as he grew older, I had to schedule when he went outside for exercise. I tried to walk Sona for an hour every day, which was good not only for him but also for me! In New York City, you often see a dog walker sauntering down the street with six or eight dogs on leashes, all quite disciplined (even the humans!), out for their daily exercise. I always wanted Sona to join such a group, but we lived in the wrong part of town. Many dog walkers, understandably, preferred not to work in highly congested midtown Manhattan with all the pedestrians, stores, and office buildings. When work piled up and I couldn't walk Sona myself, I sniffed around quite a bit and found one willing to take Sona on solo walks in midtown. Later, Maria took on the task. I always thought that if Sona had been used to trotting along with other dogs, he would have developed a better sense of himself as part of the canine pack, instead of thinking he was a person. There were days when I felt Sona thought the only difference between him and me was that he had a couple of extra legs.

Sona wasn't wild about exercise, but he loved massages, especially in his later years, when he developed arthritis. First, he would stretch out one leg for a rub, then the other. Soon, he expected one every day after his morning walk. These "massage sessions" became our quality time together. Also, massaging your dog can help improve relaxation, oxygenation, pain relief, joint flexibility, and immune system tolerance. The internet offers good guides and advice on how to properly massage your dog. If you don't do it correctly, you can cause serious injury or aggravate a medical condition. There's also valuable information on acupuncture, chiropractic medicine, and other alternative therapies that dog owners are turning to more often these days.

As a dog ages, good grooming becomes more important. Marsha, who groomed Sona throughout his life, once told me people often say that their dogs can no longer be groomed. She tells them gently, "Your dog is just getting older, and you and your dog need to adapt to that."

Whenever Sona had an appointment with the groomer, I took him there myself and stayed to see how he was treated. Was his cage comfortable? Was he being looked after? Was the dryer the right temperature? (A cool or warm setting is best for a pet.) Was the groomer holding the nozzle a few inches away from Sona's hair and keeping the airflow in constant motion to prevent heat from concentrating in one spot and burning him?

Matted and tangled hair are known to cause a dog a lot of stress, mostly because of all the knots that pull on the dog's fur during grooming. Since Sona had become old and frail, leaving home and taking him to a groomer seemed like unnecessary stress. I opted to wash him at home in the kitchen sink! The baths took a great deal of time and patience, but I didn't mind. Between washings, I helped maintain a healthy coat by brushing Sona every day. Plenty of products are available for the home groomer—dog shampoos and conditioners, brushes, and nail clippers. I often used regular baby shampoo because it was what Sona seemed to prefer.

I confess, though, that I didn't give Sona the best baths. He much preferred that Maria bathe him. I think he sensed I was overprotective and a little nervous about the whole process, which added to his own anxiety. Sona trusted Maria completely and was very compliant with her. If I wanted to cut the hair on his ears, he was likely to growl at me, as if to say, "Stop, you!" But when Maria approached to clean out his ears and cut the matted hair under his legs, he never objected. He would even lick her hands while she petted him and told him how much she loved him and how fabulous he would look after his bath was over. Maria, who was raised in Quito, Ecuador, spoke to him in Spanish. "Venga, mi amor," she would say. Maybe, I thought, with Sona learning Irish from the Gallaghers and Spanish from Maria, I could now have a trilingual dog!

Gym Fit

If you want to keep your pet in good shape or help him drop those extra pounds, have you considered taking your pooch to a gym for animals? Structured fitness programs are becoming more common as animals face increasing risk of health issues such as orthopedic, respiratory, circulatory, and heart problems, not to mention diabetes, pancreatic disorders, and joint and liver disease. Regular gym visits offer a more disciplined exercise program than most owners can manage alone or have the time for.

To determine whether it's time for your dog to hit the gym, run your hand along his side. If you can't feel his ribs, it's time to go. Fitness gyms for dogs run the gamut from small, family-owned businesses to larger and more full-scale facilities. Typically, a fitness gym might include treadmills, balance platforms, and exercise or stability balls specifically designed for dogs to help build their leg muscles. Some gyms will also provide indoor swimming pools and agility training with jumps, hoops, tunnels, balance beams, and weave posts. There are reports that, through disciplined exercise, dogs that are 50 pounds overweight were able to trim as much as 27 pounds off in one year. However, it requires a determined owner and a disciplined dog to pull that off.

If you feel guilty about going to the gym and leaving your dog at home, you may be able to take him with you. Why not try to find a personal trainer who can work with you and your dog? That's the idea behind Go Fetch Run, which shut down because of Covid-19 but plans to start offering group as well as private personal training sessions soon for you and your pup in San Antonio, Texas (angela-aramburu.squarespace.com).

- 8 -

Help for Aging Dogs

In today's digital world and expanding health care market, many products are available for dogs suffering from various kinds of handicaps. You can find these products at Walkin' Pets (www.handicappedpets.com). Another organization worth knowing about is the Handicapped Pets Foundation (www.hpets.org), which raises money to equip handicapped dogs with whatever they need, and to aid in pet mobility. Using aids acknowledges that a dog's abilities are declining and that the eventual end is inevitable, but it can also make the last months, or even years, happier and more comfortable for both the dog and the owner.

As your dog gets older, you will have to spend more time on his or her health care needs.

Even if a dog is in relatively good health throughout his life, it's a good idea to take him to the vet for a yearly geriatric work-up, which can help spotlight underlying health problems.

Jonathan Cooper, DVM, at the Westbury Animal Hospital in Houston, Texas, offers a wellness program for senior pets: Dogs come in every six months for a regular checkup, and every year, the dog also gets a urinalysis, complete blood count, and chemistry profile. "If we can pick up a change in kidney function early in the process, we can get the dog on a proper sodium-restricted diet. And we can catch some types of cancer before they've had an opportunity to spread," Dr. Cooper told me. "Many diseases can be picked up early, before they get to be a problem, with good regular physical exams." I thought that was a great idea and made sure Sona went to his vet at least every six months for checkups.

To make life easier for you, periodically check your home to see if you can find ways to make life more comfortable for your aging pet. I used to think about my home from Sona's perspective. If I was unable to do a lot for myself, what would I want? Would I like that shiny kitchen floor if I had arthritis or hip dysplasia? Probably not, so why expect that a dog will feel differently? One of the first things I did was install slate on the floor in my kitchen, where Sona spent a lot of time. An easily negotiated pathway from the food, to the bed, to the door, to the outside is also important for older dogs.

I have a friend who, as her rather large mixed Labrador got older, gradually found herself picking the dog up and carrying her around. First it was just up or down steep sets of stairs; then eventually, it was any stairs at all, even a couple of shallow stairs that led to an outside porch. Soon, she said even a slow stroll around the block required several rescues, where she would have to lift her dog back onto her feet after her dog had stumbled. Each time, my friend said, the dog looked at her as if to apologize for all the trouble, but also to acknowledge she was grateful for the help. I told my friend about special equipment that could be useful for disabled dogs.

When Your Pet Can't Walk or Has Trouble Walking

Whether your pet is temporarily injured or permanently disabled, a paralyzed or semi-paralyzed animal can still gain some mobility and freedom, thanks to advances in animal care equipment. Once your pet has adapted to his mobility device, he can navigate the world on his own and regain some sense of independence.

1 - Help your dog stay mobile.

An orthopedic walkabout harness that helps lift a dog to its feet, a specialized wheelchair, a dog sling that provides support to your pet's front or hind legs, and pet ramps to go up and down stairs can help your dog get around. Monitor all pet devices to make sure they are fitted correctly and function properly so that they don't harm your pet in any way, including irritating the skin.

2 - Go to dog therapy.

If your dog has had an injury, suffers from pain from arthritis, or is getting old, rehabilitation therapy can offer great help. Such therapies include chiropractic massage, acupuncture, swimming, and therapeutic exercises, all done under the care of a qualified canine rehabilitation veterinarian or technician. You can find out more about dog massage at American Kennel Club (www.akc.org). Some books that also address the subject include *A Dog Lover's Guide to Canine Massage*, *The Well-Connected Dog, A Guide to Canine Acupressure*, and *Canine Massage: A Complete Reference Manual*.

3 - Stay close to your dog.

If your dog can't move quickly, having you there will give him confidence, even a feeling that he can still do things despite his limitations. If you move from room to room, help your dog to go with you. Encourage play sessions with you or your family members. All this will help improve his quality of life, especially if done with love and patience.

I knew that if Sona was relatively happy and enjoying his life, despite various ailments, there were many ways I could help maximize the quality of his life. If you approach the situation with creativity, compassion, and patience, you'll be surprised at the ingenious solutions you may come up with, and the degree to which people around you will also contribute to helping you and your dog manage and enjoy your time together, right through until the end.

One decision most dog owners eventually face is whether to pursue advanced treatment for an aging pet, and how much that will affect the animal's quality of life. "Sometimes you need to think about whether you are going to put this animal through major invasive surgery when it probably only has a few more months to live," Dr. Han once told me. "For some people, another year or six months, or two years of quality life for their pet is worth it, whatever the cost."

In the last year of his life, Sona had to take Lasix, a diuretic, to help with his heart and kidney problems. As a result, he had to urinate every three hours except -fortunately! - at night when he was sleeping. I quickly figured out how to deal with that dicey situation rather than get upset about it. Because I'd already covered the wooden floors and rugs with the kind of rubber padding normally used under carpets, it was so easy just to wash it whenever there was an accident. I became very good at mopping - Lysol All-Purpose Cleaner, Clorox disinfecting wipes, Nature's Miracle, and a Quickie Sponge Mop became my best friends.

At one point I considered using doggie disposable diapers on Sona, but I soon realized that would lead to him developing a rash. I figured it was better just to wash and wipe his little butt whenever necessary. The first couple of times I did it, I thought, "I can't believe I'm doing this," but quick butt wipes became part of our routine, and soon I didn't give it a second thought.

Of course, it wasn't just my apartment that had to be protected from accidents and stains. There was the inconvenient reality that I lived in an apartment building in Manhattan. This meant that for me to get Sona outside, we had to negotiate a relatively long hallway, wait for an elevator, and then make it through a series of floor stops, all the way to the ground floor. Then we had to make our way across the polished tile floor of the lobby and out the door. Doing this successfully, without a mishap, became increasingly difficult the older and sicker Sona became. But he was always a well-loved dog, and in this case, the building community rose to the occasion and helped us find a way to meet the challenge.

For example, Richard Orth, a building staff member, devised a "magic carpet" for Sona that consisted of a plastic carpet runner with a string attached to it, which we rolled out in front of "His Highness," as Richard called him. I would put Sona on his magic carpet and pull him to the elevator. When we returned from the yard, I rolled the carpet back up and kept it ready and available for the next emergency. Sona got quite used to traveling on his carpet and would often wait impatiently for me to pull the rug and move him along.

My worst experience with Sona and the rug happened one day in the hallway, where a beautiful new carpet had just been laid down. I was trying to get Sona to the yard without any accidents. We rode on his magic carpet to the elevator, but as we were waiting for the elevator to arrive, Sona stepped off his rug. Just as my neighbor opened his apartment door to say hello, Sona peed on the hall carpet. The neighbor looked on in astonishment. "You didn't see that," I told him. "You did not see that!" He smiled and closed his door while I ran back to my apartment for my bottle of Nature's Miracle.

After that, whenever we rode down in the elevator, I had Sona sit on the carpet the entire time, on the theory he couldn't urinate if he wasn't standing. It always amazed me that by the time we got to the door in the basement, Sona would stand up, often wobbly, and move ever so slowly to the backyard, even though, by this point, he was completely blind. He had learned how to manage the steps to get outside. He would tap his paws in front of him to guide himself. He would then pee, and take about 15 minutes to poop, sometimes just going around in circles until he was ready to make a deposit.

For the most part, these visits out to the backyard worked well ... unless it was storming. Thank God for big umbrellas and Sona's small yellow raincoat. Those morning walks were often when I had my most creative ideas for projects. My thinking seemed to unclog while I was following Sona around the yard and waiting for him to answer nature's call.

After we returned from those morning visits to the backyard, I would feed Sona. Due to his advanced age, it took about an hour to both feed and walk him. I tried to do this by 8:30 every morning, even though I woke up every night at 3 a.m. to check on him and make sure the apartment wasn't too hot or cold, to turn the air conditioners up or down; to close windows; to make sure he hadn't peed or pooped and was lying helplessly in his own waste. If he was, I would clean him up and wipe his paws. As I did this, he would stand there and sometimes his expression seemed to say, "Look, Mom, you missed a spot." One lucky break? Although Sona was a "guy," he always squatted to pee. Can you imagine how different the above story might have been if he'd hoisted a leg up and sprayed?

It's true that near the end of his life, my schedule for taking care of Sona was demanding by any standard, so much so that I had to make a list of his medications, organize the pills by time of day, and post the list on the kitchen wall. My daily routine with Sona looked something like this:

> **8:30 a.m.:** Go downstairs for Sona's bathroom break, then breakfast and medications.
>
> **12 p.m.:** Back downstairs for another bathroom break, then lunch and medications.
>
> **4 p.m.:** Another bathroom break.
>
> **6-7 p.m.:** Snacks and medications.
>
> **9:45 p.m.:** Last trip downstairs to the backyard, then final medications.

Because of the rigor of this schedule, I never could sleep later than 8:30 a.m. or go to bed before 10 p.m. Yes, I was often exhausted, but I was never resentful about the time I had to put into Sona's care. Although caring for Sona was a major commitment, especially in the end stages of his life, he was also, in many ways, my salvation, my solace from worries and work. Maybe that's what unconditional love is all about: Whether it's a human being or an animal, we're blessed when we have someone in our lives to love and commit to rather than focusing on ourselves.

As Sona's strength began to ebb away, he would come up to the apartment from the yard and lie down in the foyer, as if he were too weary to take another step. I would often lie down on the floor beside him, petting him, talking to him, and trying to soothe him as best I could. Eventually, he could no longer lift his leg so that I could rub his tummy, the way he'd liked so much over the years. He couldn't even lick my hands! I remember one day just lying on the floor near him, tears flowing, crying and saying, "Oh, Sona, I know I'm losing you." Yet as sad as those memories are, I'm grateful I had the opportunity for a long, slow goodbye. Some owners whose pets die suddenly or violently are not so lucky.

Another issue that arises when you have an aging dog, in addition to the cost of health care, and your ability to pay, is whether to euthanize your pet. While this would be unthinkable for many dog owners who prioritize their pet's health care above anything else, for most dog owners, the question of euthanasia remains a tough one. The American Veterinary Medical Association suggests asking yourself the question, "Does my pet have more bad days than good days?" to help you make the decision.

A friend of mine, a strong and very active but petite woman, who found herself carrying her big 12-year-old Golden Retriever around more and more often as time went on, asked her vet, "How long should I continue to do this?" She told me the vet's wise answer. "As long as that tail keeps wagging," he had said, adding with a kind and sympathetic look, "and as long as you want to." She knew that her vet understood the bond that existed between her and her Golden Retriever and could also evaluate the dog's condition and behavior such as whether he was spending more time alone, sleeping more than usual and losing weight.

Stephanie LaFarge, Ph.D., a psychologist, was formerly the senior director of counseling services at the American Society for the Prevention of Cruelty to Animals (ASPCA). While there, she ran a 24-hour pet loss support hotline that received more than 3,000 calls a year. She estimated that about half of the calls came from pet owners who were grieving over an animal that had died, and the other half were from people who had an animal still alive and suffering, trying to decide when to euthanize. LaFarge explained that many of these pet owners, despite whether their animal was suffering or not, mentioned that they "didn't want to play God" when facing the question of euthanasia. "But in some states, failure to euthanize at the end of life when the animal is dying is considered animal cruelty and is illegal," she said. "You are killing your animal with the intention of stopping the suffering. People get so caught up in how sad and guilty they feel about what they are doing, they lose sight of what the animal feels.

The person who doesn't give a hoot puts the dog in the backyard and waits for it to die. We're socialized not to euthanize, but it's often the kindest thing you can do."

From a personal standpoint, watching Sona and learning from his example made me realize that what applies to older dogs may have a similar truth for older people as well. In our society, we're too quick to dismiss the elderly, saying, "Oh, they are past their time. They can't really contribute anymore." Pope Francis, on a trip to Sardinia, spoke movingly of older people when he said globalization had caused a culture where the weakest in society suffered the most, and that often those on the fringes, including the elderly, "fall away." He said they were victims of a "hidden euthanasia" caused by neglect of those no longer considered productive.

Who's to say what limits we should place on the elderly? If we, as a society, don't write them off so casually, maybe they'll figure life is worth living and hang in there a little longer, as long as they're not suffering extreme pain. A positive attitude can conquer overwhelming circumstances. It's an important lesson I learned from Sona, and one I will never forget.

Is Your Dog Helping You to Live Longer?

According to a 2017 Swedish study published in Scientific Reports, if you live alone and own a dog, you can decrease your risk of death by 33 percent and your risk of cardiovascular disease related to death by 36 percent when compared with single individuals without a pet. Chances of a heart attack decreased by 11 percent.

If you live in a multi-person household and own a dog, risk of death fell 11 percent, and the chances of dying from cardiovascular disease were 15 percent lower. Experts believe these health benefits are correlated with increased physical activity among dog owners, including taking the pet out for daily walks. There was also an increased sense of social well-being among pet owners, which can decrease stress and increase immune system development. Owners of hunting breeds such as terriers, retrievers, and scent hounds saw the biggest health benefits, possibly because those breeds tend to be among the most active.

- 9 -

"Don't Worry, Your Dog Will Show You How"

I was surprised when Sona developed glaucoma during his first year of life. Glaucoma occurs when pressure on the eye causes inadequate fluid drainage. I was horrified when I learned that such eye problems were typical for Cocker Spaniels, and that glaucoma was one of the most challenging eye diseases faced by veterinarians. Fully 40 percent of dogs with glaucoma can become blind in the affected eye within the first year, whether they have medical or surgical treatment or not. Sona faced that challenge, though not for many years to come.

Stephen Gross, VMD, Sona's ophthalmologist for most of his life, explained how such serious eye diseases can happen so early in certain dog breeds. "All you need is one very good show dog winning a lot of awards and at a very young age," he told me. "Breeders use these dogs to reproduce so they will have a lot of puppies. Later, they find out that the dog has a major health issue of some sort, but by then, the genes have been already transmitted to many future generations of dogs. That's why you see more glaucoma in a certain line of dogs."

Gentle and patient, Dr. Gross was on the staff at the Matthew J. Ryan Veterinary Hospital of the University of Pennsylvania, yet he traveled once a week to New York City to see his patients here. Each month, I took Sona to Dr. Gross to check his eye pressure and get prescriptions for medicines to keep the glaucoma under control. Dr. Gross taught me how to recognize the warning signs that indicated if the pressure was getting too high: if Sona began rubbing his eye, or holding it shut; if his eyes were red; or if he just seemed uncharacteristically subdued. Other than that, we started every day with eyedrops, which helped control the eye pressure, and Sona led a very normal life otherwise.

When Sona lost vision in his left eye when he was 13, I was traumatized. "How can I handle this?" I asked Dr. Gross. I'll never forgot his answer. "Don't worry," he said. "Your dog will show you how."

As time passed, I found this was true. "Most dogs do amazingly well with the loss of vision," Dr. Gross told me. "The first few days with no vision is sometimes hard, but it's pretty amazing how well they start to compensate by using their other senses." He admitted later that when Sona went blind, he was less worried about how Sona would cope than how I would.

But once I started following Sona's lead, I did just fine, too. Dr. Gross's words became my mantra. I kept telling everyone, "Sona will show us, Sona will show us." Sona did manage to hold on to some vision in his right eye for another year: He didn't turn fully blind until he was around 14 years old.

When treating Sona's blindness, I used two kinds of eye-drops, Timoptic and Xalatan, the same medicine used for humans. Toward the end of his life, he could no longer tolerate Timoptic because of his heart condition (Timoptic can slow the heartbeat and alter blood pressure), so we switched to Pilocar and Cosopt. To keep his eyes lubricated, I also used Hylashield ointment. Fortunately, Sona was always good about having the drops put in his eyes. He would sit down and lift his head up, as if to say, "All right, I'm ready. Bring it on."

I fought so hard to save as much of Sona's sight as possible, knowing that even if he could only see shapes, it would make a difference in his life and enable him to remain relatively independent. "You just did it," Dr. Gross remembered. "Some people simply make the decision, 'We can't afford to do that,' and that's that. Or, 'We don't have time to do that.' Or 'We don't want to do that.' But people like you are just so dedicated to the pet that's become a family member."

As I adapted to the reality that Sona would eventually go totally blind, I decided I needed to get in front of the problem as soon as possible. I wanted to imagine

Sona's world and understand what it would be like to live without any vision, after having been able to see for so many years. How lonely and frightening it must be, even for a little dog with such a fighting spirit.

To prepare myself for the inevitable, I read a book about coping with blind dogs. I also called in a dog trainer, a specialist in this area, to come to my apartment to see how I could make it easier for Sona to move around.

By this time, Sona had also gone deaf. Can you imagine how difficult it must have been for a dog to lose two important senses, to be both blind and deaf at the same time? There were limits to how much we could help him. Sound signals to guide him were not a possibility, but I hoped that by using vanilla syrup to create a path along the floor, we might train him to "follow his nose" and walk in the same area all the time. Although smell is usually the last sense to go for a dog, Sona never really got the hang of "the vanilla walk," so I had to continue searching for other solutions.

In search of more ideas to make my apartment more manageable for Sona, I asked a veterinarian who had two blind dogs of her own to help me figure out how I could alter my living space. Some of the solutions we came up with were simple ones, such as keeping his water bowl and feeding dish in the same spot, so he would know where to find them. Other solutions were more involved and imaginative. I bought big rolls of bubble wrap at Staples and placed it along the lower part of the walls and against jagged objects so that if Sona bumped into something, he wouldn't hurt himself. I wasn't beyond getting on all fours to look for any hazards. Admittedly, the apartment didn't look as nice as it normally did, but I didn't care. Sona's comfort and mobility were what mattered.

Everyone made a habit of walking close to Sona, so that he could smell and feel our presence and sense the vibration of our walking. We just kept asking ourselves, "What will make the difference for Sona?" One answer, of course, was a lot of attention and reassurance through hugs and petting, which turned out to be equally therapeutic for both of us.

I also contacted a woman I knew whose dog had lost his vision by the time he was 10. When the dog first became blind, people asked her, "Are you going to put him to sleep? He can't see." She told me the thought had never crossed her mind. "The most important thing is to be patient," she said. "You have to remember none of this is the dog's fault."

I encourage anyone thinking of adopting a dog from a shelter to consider adopting a blind or deaf dog. Disabled dogs can be just as valuable as able pets. I remember reading the story of a blind and deaf three-legged dog named True, who lived in Grady County, Oklahoma.

True saved his family by waking them up at night so that they could escape a burning house. The fire had been started by an electrical short circuit, and True, despite his limitations, sensed the danger and responded accordingly. A disabled dog has so much to offer and can make a real difference in your life, teaching you about unconditional love, how to share challenges, how to be creative, and how to appreciate all the important gifts life has to offer.

Dr. Gross was right. They will show you how.

When Your Pet Is Blind

A dog's dominant sense is smell rather than vision, which is one reason some owners aren't aware at first that their pet has gone blind. Whether your pet was born blind or became blind from age or disease, there are several steps you can take to make your pet feel at ease:

1 - Talk to your pet.

Your voice is soothing and will help identify you for a dog that might be anxious or even fearful in the beginning. Dogs can soon adjust to their condition with lots of help, love, and patience from family members.

2 - Rely on your dog's sense of smell.

Even though your dog may be blind, he still has a good nose. No wonder dogs are used to detect bombs and drugs and even illnesses such as cancer in humans. One way to keep his sniffing ability sharp is to hide treats with distinctive scents inside his toys and watch your pet go for it.

3 - Keep your furniture in place.

It's usually best not to rearrange your furniture, so your pet can memorize the layout of a room. If you do need to move anything, make sure you lead your pet around the new layout a few times before leaving him alone.

4 - Keep floors and passageways clear.

Stray toys, blankets, and backpacks tossed on the floor can confuse your pet and, in some cases, even be hazardous.

5 - Dog-proof your yard.

Fence off any areas that could be dangerous, such as a pool or a path that leads to the road. Also check for any holes in the ground, and trim your plants, so they won't damage your dog's eyes.

6 - Keep your dog active.

Just because your dog is disabled does not mean he shouldn't maintain an active social life. Serve as your dog's eyes when you take him out, paying special attention to avoid aggressive dogs.

When Your Pet Is Deaf

A hearing-impaired pet needs to be trained through hand signals rather than voice commands. Here are some tips to keep your hearing-impaired dog safe.

1 - Pay attention to your dog's hearing.

Dogs, of course, don't tell you they are going deaf. Sometimes you have to make a noise to get your dog's attention and if there is no response it's time to check with your vet for the cause. There are many reasons your dog could become deaf, including congenital defects, chronic ear infections, head injuries, and old age. Some breeds, including Australian Shepherds, Dalmatians, Great Danes, and Cocker Spaniels, are notably susceptible.

2 - Track your dog.

There are lots of ways to do this. You could simply attach a bell or light to your dog's collar, but you could also go high-tech and hang a GPS tracker next to his dog tags or install a high definition video camera that comes with night vision. There are also dog tags you can hang from your pet's collar that say, "I am deaf," to let people know.

3 - Let him know you're there.

Never startle your dog. If your dog can't hear you, making eye contact or giving him a gentle touch will let him know of your presence. He could also become tuned in to the vibration of your footsteps. You can also train your dog to look at you by turning a flashlight on and off and then rewarding him when he comes to you.

4 - Use hand signals.

You'll need to find a new way to communicate with your dog. Typical hand signals include lowering your hand to indicate that a dog should lie down, raising your hand to tell him to stay, putting your fingers to your lips to tell him its dinner time, and pointing to the ground to say "no" or "stop."

- 10 -

When It's Time to Say Goodbye

"My dog's pressure in the right eye is 80; in the left eye it's 40," I said to the reservation agent on the phone that Friday afternoon. "That's much too high, and he can't see or hear. I've just come from the vet. I need your help."

I was supposed be on a midday flight from Newark to Chicago the next day, but now I needed to fly out much later. As soon as the agent pulled up my reservation, she understood my predicament. I had a round-trip ticket that had been purchased months earlier for $236. Now, with a last-minute change, I was facing the possibility of paying nearly $1,400 if I rebooked the flight at the last minute.

The ticket agent heard in my voice my very real concerns about staying in the city to be with my sick dog as well as the high cost involved with changing flight plans. "I know how you feel," she said. "I have a Lab that we just lost in March. He had cancer." That opened a conversation between us. We spent about 15 minutes talking about her dog, how her family had tried to save him, and how they had all gathered together to be at his side when it was time to put him to sleep. "The most important thing is for you to be able to hold him," she said.

I then told her about Sona. It all started that June day in 2002 when Sona didn't eat much of his lunch. He just closed his mouth and wouldn't take any more food. At first Maria, who knew Sona so well, thought he wasn't hungry. But when I tried to give him dinner later in the day, again he wouldn't eat. I can still see him refusing to open his mouth and turning his face away. That was a big red flag. Sona lived by his stomach, and for him not to be tempted to eat threw me into a tailspin. I took that as a clear signal he wasn't well.

After the agent heard my story, she changed my reservation so that I could leave town later the next day, and she didn't charge me anything extra! I remember once a travel agent had said to me, in talking about airfares, "The early bird gets the worm." This time I thought, "Well, a dog lover can also help you get the worm. Bless her!"

When you have a sick dog, you always think you'll be prepared for when he is no longer with you. In Sona's case, it all happened so quickly that it came as a shock. My friends, doctors, and I had fought for Sona's life so many times before—we wanted him to live as many days as he could, if he was comfortable and not in pain. When the end finally arrived, we thought it was just another emergency we could work through. How often had we gone through similar situations? How many trips had we made to the Animal Medical Center with Sona in tow, ready to combat another health scare? Each time we'd done this over the years, the little fighter had pulled through, again and again.

But not this time.

I didn't know at the time that not eating was often a sign a dog's body might be shutting down. All I knew was that Sona took his medications with his food, so if he wasn't eating, he also wasn't getting medicated. Since I thought he was just being picky, I reverted to the old familiar tricks I'd used over the years to get him to eat. I mixed his regular food with cottage cheese. When that didn't work, I gave him a little Gerber's baby food. He still didn't budge. I then offered him the ultimate temptation: a piece of chicken and fresh bread. He refused it.

When it dawned on me that something was drastically wrong, I called Dr. Solomon. Although it was after office hours, Dr. Solomon asked me to describe how Sona was acting.

"He just won't eat," I said.

Dr. Solomon paused on the other end of the line. "Try and get his most important pressure pill in his mouth, monitor him, and bring him in first thing in the morning," he told me.

When I couldn't even open Sona's mouth to give him the pill, I called Maria. "Was Sona all right at lunch?" I asked her.

"He was good, but he didn't eat all of his lunch." When I mentioned how worried I was that he wasn't eating at all now, Maria said, "I'm coming over. Maybe he'll eat for me."

By the time I got off the phone, Sona was panting a lot, walking back and forth, bumping into things, going into areas he normally would not go, drinking a lot of water, and pooping frequently. In addition to not eating, he was clearly in distress. I tried hugging and comforting him, but he just kept walking around and panting.

When Maria arrived, she scooped him into her arms. He was noticeably trembling. "He's really sick," she told me. "We go to the doctor."

I called Dr. Solomon again, and said we were very concerned about Sona and didn't want to wait until morning to bring him in. "I'll meet you at the clinic," he said. This was around 8 p.m.

We quickly gathered all Sona's medicines, wrapped him in his favorite blanket, and rushed to Dr. Solomon's office. When we arrived, the doctor hurriedly took Sona into the examining room while we anxiously waited outside. I couldn't help but remember all the times I'd been here with Sona. This veterinary clinic was like a second home to him.

Dr. Solomon later told me he'd been most concerned about pneumonia, kidney issues, and Sona's eye. The problem turned out to be Sona's eye pressure, which had shot up dangerously high and was causing him extreme pain. He also had a fever of 104 degrees. The doctor felt he could stabilize Sona and suggested that I wait until morning to see whether I could fly out on my planned trip to Chicago.

When I visited Sona early Saturday morning, he was doing so much better that I decided to leave for Chicago that afternoon. He was still quite sick, but his condition was not as critical as it had been. All I had to do in Chicago was attend one board meeting, and then I'd be back in New York City late the next day.

Throughout Saturday and Sunday, I called to check on Sona every few hours. He was weak but holding his own. But when I called on Monday morning, after I'd returned to New York and was anxious to see Sona, Dr. Solomon sounded worried and sad. I could hear in his voice that he was extremely nervous about Sona's deteriorating condition. He told me the eye pressure was down and had stabilized, but Sona had dropped from 26 to 23 pounds in a matter of days, roughly 12 percent of his body weight. "We might win the battle and lose the war," he told me, and my heart caught in my chest. Was he really suggesting what I thought he was? "Our boy is not looking well," he added.

"Is it like Sona is shutting down?" I asked, my voice shaking.

"It could be," he said quietly.

When Maria and I went to visit Sona on Monday afternoon, he appeared to be more comfortable than Dr. Solomon's description earlier in the day. The fever had broken, and he didn't seem to be in pain, but he still wasn't eating. I clung to the idea that if we could get him to start eating again, he'd be okay. Back at home, I prayed that Sona would pull through one more time, the way he always had before.

I couldn't wait for the next morning to see Sona again. I was clearly expecting him to be better, but once Maria and I arrived, we found that he'd taken another turn for the worse. Dr. Solomon brought him into the room, wrapped in a blue towel. Sona looked so lifeless, his eyes unfocused, and he was still panting a great deal. His fever had spiked up again. Over the years, Sona dealt with so many health issues that it was hard to determine what was causing his problems now. Our best guess was that he was experiencing a complete medical breakdown. Through my tears I saw the expression on Dr. Solomon's face, and I could see his anguish when he said, "I think it's time."

I felt a raw ache in my throat. I understood what Dr. Solomon was telling me. We had always said that we'd never use heroic means on Sona, because any sort of surgery would require anesthesia, a definite danger for a dog with heart problems. Briefly, I considered feeding Sona with a tube, which might extend his life for a few weeks or even months, but at what quality? If Sona, the voracious eater, the dog who savored every morsel, wasn't eating, maybe it was his way of telling us something we should listen to. Perhaps he, too, was saying, "It's time."

Dr. Solomon said, "I'm going to leave you and Maria with Sona, so you can have time alone with him." He was telling us we should say goodbye. As the reality dawned on me, the pain was almost unbearable. We had only been at Dr. Solomon's office for about an hour, and we were already faced with ending Sona's life! I couldn't believe it. The fragile threads that had held Sona's life together for so many years were breaking, hope was turning to despair, and the finality of it was all so real.

Maria and I took some tissues, wet them and kept wiping Sona's mouth to give him comfort. I rested my head on his chest, rubbed him and said, "Oh, Sona, I love you so!" I knew he couldn't see or hear me, but maybe he could at least feel the vibrations of my hand. I wanted so much for him to know he wasn't alone, that we were there and would love him until the very end. By this point, Maria and I were both crying. When Dr. Solomon came back into the room to put Sona to sleep, Maria was in such despair that she hurried out of the room.

I knew I had to stay with Sona as he crossed over from life into death. Dr. Solomon's presence helped to give me strength for the ordeal ahead. Although he was outwardly calm, I knew that he, too, was devastated. He'd been his vet for Sona's entire life, from the time he was a captivating puppy through all the years of his illnesses. Dr. Solomon had been there for the good times as well as the heartbreakers. Often, if I was away for a day, Sona would stay at Dr. Solomon's office. I think he saw it as his private daycare center. The staff loved him, a little puppy-in-charge, with full run of the place, greeting other dogs as they came in for their own appointments. If Sona had a health problem outside Dr. Solomon's area of expertise, he would refer us to the appropriate specialist, but he was always consulting on the case, checking to make sure Sona was getting the best care possible. I knew, as we were together in the room now at the end of Sona's life, we would be comforting each other.

Surprisingly, most pet owners don't want to stay with their pet through the death process. I read a vet's story in the Daily Mail that claimed the hardest part of his job was when he had to put an animal down without the pet's owner in the room. According to this vet, as many as 90 percent of owners don't want to stay when their pet is given the injection that will end the animal's life. As a result, the animal's last moments are spent frantically looking around for their owners. They are scared in this unfamiliar environment and don't understand why they were left behind.

First, Dr. Solomon gave Sona a shot of Valium. Then he gave a second shot that causes a loss of consciousness within seconds, followed by depression of the respiratory system and cardiac arrest. Throughout this procedure, Sona didn't move. It was as if he'd gone to sleep. I remember thinking how peaceful the whole process was, and that provided some comfort.

Still, after Sona left me, all I could do was hold him and cry. There seemed no end to the grief, the sense of profound loss. Finally, Dr. Solomon said, "We'll cremate him. Do you want his ashes?"

I was probably still in shock because I didn't know how to answer. For a journalist, someone who could always talk, I suddenly found I couldn't say much of anything. My throat had closed up. Every word was an effort. Dr. Solomon opened a cabinet and pointed to two urns. "This is Cathy, and this is VC," he said. Cathy, a rescued mixed breed with three legs, and VC were his two favorite dogs, and to my surprise, their remains had been with him in his office for all these years.

I looked up from Sona's body and stared at the urns. "Is it all right if Sona stays with them for a while?" I asked.

He didn't even hesitate. Sona's ashes were placed in an urn and stored next to Cathy and VC. I'm so grateful I made that choice.

For a long time after Sona's death, I wondered repeatedly whether I should have gone to Chicago just before Sona's death. Maybe I should have stayed with him every day while he was in the hospital. He could have smelled my presence, and maybe that would have given him the strength necessary to continue fighting a little longer. Even now, years later, I still ask myself a question many pet owners agonize over after losing a pet: *Could I have done more?*

When I returned to my apartment after Sona's death—an apartment where we had lived together for 15 years—the loneliness was overwhelming. The apartment felt so silent. I started sobbing, and as much as I tried, couldn't get hold of myself. This little four-legged dynamo, despite his various illnesses, and with his winning personality and loving heart so much larger than he was, had become such a vital and uplifting part of my life. Sona had known the men I'd loved, sometimes weighing in with a growl of disapproval, and he'd known my family and all my friends. Even better, he had his own circle of people he'd cultivated over the years. Suddenly a space that had seemed so right for the two of us—this home we shared—felt so empty. Living with Sona, in so many ways, had been like sharing a home with another person. There were whole areas of the apartment that were his alone: the space for his bed, his walking areas, the corner of the kitchen where he ate, the places where he liked to stretch out and rest. His toys and food dishes were still around, but he was not. And I couldn't bring myself to throw out his magic carpet. I stashed it away in a closet, and it's still there to this day.

For a while, I was overwhelmed with memories. I recalled how whenever I returned to the apartment, the first thing I would do is check on Sona to make sure he was all right. Then I'd immediately put on his harness and take him outside to the yard for a walk. I remembered how, when Sona was still a puppy and I would return home from work, he would tremble with excitement, without fail, wagging his tail, ready to grab my scarf if I were wearing one and tug on it. I would reach down and hug him, feeling his energy shake through my arms. Next, he would lie on his back, paws in the air, wagging his tail even more furiously, and wait for me to rub his legs and tummy. He would lick me wherever he could, on my face, my hands, my arms. Sometimes I wondered what he would do if I licked him back.

Now, when I returned to the apartment, I felt aimless. I didn't have Sona to check on, or for him to check on me and cheer me up if I was in a down mood. I had to face, alone, the silence and my memories as I thought back on the joy and unconditional love that Sona had given not only to me but also to so many other people. While it was true that Sona required a good deal of extra care and was often quite sick, I never regretted or resented the time and cost I'd put into helping him feel better. I'd do it all over again if given the chance.

After Sona's death, I was flooded with calls and letters from friends offering their help, concern, and sympathy. In an age of emails, it was a reminder of how important and moving old-fashioned communication can be. A handwritten note or a personal telephone call lightened my pain and uplifted my spirit. I remember one friend's response in particular, "Cry with tears to wash the mossy stone clean, down to the bare rock so new moss can grow." Then she added, "A burial, with flowers and tears, for closure. Half a bottle of red. A shoulder to cry on."

I remember reading before Sona's death something actor Jean-Claude Van Damme said when he lost his dog: Accepting his pet's death was just as difficult as losing a family member. I felt much the same way. I had held my mother when she passed away, just as I'd done with Sona.

The depth of loss I felt was similar in both cases. Some people might say, "How can you compare the death of a dog to the death of a parent?" But such naysayers are likely not dog owners. In the end, how do you quantify love? How do you say that one kind of love is more important than another? The losses of both my mother and Sona were so difficult to bear, in different ways.

After Sona died, I worried about his buddies, Martha and John. They had loved him so much. "At first there was sadness, because Sona wouldn't be here anymore," Martha told me. "But we were wrong about that, because Sona's spirit lives on in our house. John and I talk about him all the time. We remember all the funny things he did." Martha also mentioned that toward the end of Sona's life, she felt Sona was ready to go, and was, in his own way, preparing us for his inevitable departure. "He had the animal instinct, which is probably better than humans," she said. "He just kind of wanted to say goodbye and go to sleep." She felt Sona had been ready to die for a while before he did, but that he was waiting until we were ready as well. "Sona always gave as much love as we gave him," she said. Then she laughed and added, "His was done with a lick and a slobber. You knew, when you saw his face light up and he wagged his tail, that was Sona's hug."

- 1 1 -

Moving On

People process their grief over the loss of a pet in several different ways. For some, having a grave—a specific place to visit—can offer comfort, while others might prefer placing their pet's cremated remains in a special area of the house. As I was moving through the grieving process, I created a scrapbook, in which I captured many of the memorable events in my life with Sona. I remembered what the English novelist and poet George Eliot said: "Our dead are never dead to us until we have forgotten them." As time passed, I could always go back to the book, page through it, and remember the countless ways in which Sona had brought me joy. The book helped ease my sadness and replace it with joyful memories, often full of laughter.

    I told an Italian friend how painful it was for me without Sona and how much I missed him. My friend suggested a unique way I could cherish his memory. "Why don't you a plant a tree in the backyard of your apartment building and mix Sona's ashes in the soil?" she asked. "That way he will always be there with you."

Although I had left Sona's remains in an urn next to VC and Cathy in Dr. Solomon's office, I understood the appeal of associating death with a living tree. Another option is to have your pet's ashes mingled with yours. The right to do so was decided in a 2013 landmark decision in the state of New York that reversed an earlier ban halting this practice. The case that resulted in the ruling involved the New York Department of State barring the then-117-year-old Hartsdale Pet Cemetery in Westchester County, New York, from burying the ashes of a retired New York Police Department officer with those of his three Maltese dogs. His niece, an attorney, championed his cause and won the right to have her uncle's ashes buried with his cherished dogs. Under the same ruling, the pet cemeteries were not allowed to charge a fee for a human burial or advertise those services.

Another way that some owners deal with moving past their grief at the loss of a pet is to get a new one. For others, this feels like a betrayal, as if they aren't loyal to the memory of the dog they've lost. "When people say they can't open their hearts again, I tell them you just haven't tried, or you're not ready to try yet," Dr. Solomon said. "But a new animal can put a whole new slice of the pie before you that you didn't even know you had. It doesn't take away from the old slice. It just gives you a new slice."

I have friends who sought out support groups to deal with their grief. As is the case when dealing with the loss of human life, a support group can serve as an effective way of sharing the pain: learning how others cope, understanding that what you are feeling is normal, and realizing that, in time, the sadness will pass. Similarly, pet loss counseling services and hotlines can also assist people through the transition process. I confessed to Dr. LaFarge, the pet psychologist, that I was having a difficult time recovering from Sona's death and asked if this was normal. "If you could turn grief on and off like a spigot, you would," she answered. "It's painful, and it's exhausting, and it is work. But you grieve according to the amount you need to grieve. And it's different for people at different ages. Sometimes parents are disappointed because their children don't react the way they think they should after a pet's death. But it's not developmentally appropriate for children to spend a lot of time stuck in grief. And sometimes for older people who are uncertain about what would happen to the animal in the case of their own death, they may be relieved that the pet didn't outlive them."

She also mentioned that people have genuine questions about what to say to grieving dog owners. "They say things like 'My friend is devastated but won't ask for help,'" LaFarge said. "'What should I do?'" That was true in my case: After Sona died, a lot of my friends struggled to know what to say to me. "You can make an opening statement like, 'I'm sorry for your loss,' which sounds like a cliché, but it gives the person a chance to talk about how they feel," LaFarge told me. "Often people will suggest getting a new dog soon. But that suggestion usually isn't welcome. It may seem like a kindhearted thing to say, but for some people, to do so would violate the sense of the uniqueness of the relationship that was lost. It's hard to say when it's time to start a new relationship with another animal. Some people are ready right away; some are not. Some are never ready."

I know from personal experience that you don't get "days off" from grief after your dog dies. You can try to push your feelings onto the back burner, but the loss is still felt, in one way or another. I would always try to tell myself, "Don't focus on grief, think of other things." Many people feel that talking about your loss and sharing and exposing your emotions are the best ways to handle grief. But everyone must trust themselves and find their own way. Some people might feel uncomfortable talking about such a personal loss, even with friends, and prefer to process the grief privately.

As I considered getting another dog, I knew that if I did, I would adopt from a shelter. At shelters you can find both purebred and mixed-breed dogs, all different ages, sizes, shapes, and personalities. Most importantly, you're adopting an abandoned animal, and in many cases saving a dog from being euthanized, a fate met by more than 600,000 dogs in the U.S. annually.

In fact, there was quite an uproar when the Obamas decided to get a playmate for their beloved Portuguese Water Dog, Bo. They called their one-year old dog Sunny because, according to reports, she was "full of energy and very affectionate." The only problem was that she apparently came from a breeder. The Obamas made a sizable donation to the Washington Humane Society in Sunny's name, but for many animal lovers that wasn't good enough. They noted that millions of shelter dogs need homes, and there was probably an adorable Portuguese Water Dog among them.

On the other hand, President Joe Biden got a dog, a handsome black and white German Shepherd named Major, from the Delaware Humane Association. But when Major moved to the White House, he began having problems, reportedly including biting incidents. Never one to give up on shelter dogs, I thought with the right training and attitude Major would work out just fine. In the meantime, he went back to Biden's home in Delaware for some catch-up.

Whenever I consider getting a shelter dog for myself, I remember Dr. Solomon's advice. "I don't care as much for the looks of a dog," he told me. "I look at the personality, whether they can be handled. Are they calm, settled, and comfortable?" He said you can judge this by the way they're interacting with other dogs and people. "Are they just a complete nervous wreck, shaking in their boots? They may be scared, but they're not aggressive, not nasty. They may be nervous, but they don't act out on it. Those are the dogs that can be worked with, who can really become very good pets."

After Sona died, relatives and friends started asking me, "Will you get another dog?" At the time, I told them I might someday, but not soon. I needed time to move on before I took on the care of a new animal. The time just hasn't been right. I realize it would take another village to help me raise a dog like Sona, and presently, running a nonprofit organization, I don't have that same extraordinary network of friends who made such a difference in the life of Sona.

Of course, not having a dog of my own right now has turned me into the lady who stops every dog on the street and immediately starts chatting like a longtime friend. Once, I was coming out of a restaurant and saw a woman sitting alone with a beautiful Labrador. I looked at the dog and he looked at me, and there was an instant connection. The woman started talking to me. I noticed that her dog was a service dog. "Oh, I'm sorry," I said. "I know I'm not supposed to get too close to your dog."

"It's all right," she told me, smiling. "I invited you into our space." It struck me that both the dog and the woman knew instinctively how much I love dogs, and they were responding to that energy.

While no dog will ever be the same for me as Sona, I understand, were it to happen, a dog could provide the focus, structure, emotional support, and happiness that Sona brought into my daily life. A Mayo Clinic study even found that people who allow their dogs to sleep in their room often have a better night. Another benefit: Dog owners often find their social lives improves if they're out with their pet. Never underestimate your dog's ability to lure people to your side for a friendly conversation. Indeed, an article in The Times of London talked about a young woman who said her male friends often wanted to borrow her Labrador. They felt the dog would make them look more appealing on their dating profiles.

One day, I may hear about a dog that needs a home or see one that is available, and when that happens, I will know, "This is the one." It could be a pedigreed dog, or a "bitza," which was how a friend once described his dog to me: "Little bitza this, and little bitza that."

Only time—and my own heart—will tell.

Adoption: One Woman's Story

Since I know next to nothing about adopting from a shelter, I turned to my cousin, Jody Joyner, who lives in New Orleans, Louisiana, for her story on how she'd adopted her Border Collie-Cocker Spaniel mix, from a shelter. She approached the task by first looking up different shelters online, searching for the type of dog she wanted. For example, Petfinder (www.petfinder.com) advertises over 250,000 adoptable pets that people can choose from. Someone interested in adopting a pet can search the Petfinder database by location, breed, size, age, gender, and other criteria, as Jody did, and learn what's involved in the adoption process. A convenient checklist outlines what bringing a new animal into the home will mean to an individual and his/her family.

Another shelter site is Animal Care Centers of NYC (www.nycacc.org) Also, there are many moving books, including *Shelter Dogs* by photographer Traer Scott (which includes photographs of 50 dogs) and *Shelter Dogs: Amazing Stories of Adopted Strays* by Peg Kehret.

"It's always good to get a rescue dog," Jody told me. When she checked Petfinder, she fell in love with one rescue dog, Sophie, almost immediately. "It was kind of a no-brainer from there," she said. "There was something about her sweet little, sad—well, maybe not sad—just her puppy face, and she had the sweetest, most beautiful eyes."

According to Jody, adopting involved a lot of paperwork. "I didn't think I was going to get her at first," she said. "But I wanted this dog so much! I thought to myself, 'This has got to work!'" Jody said she'd been asked a slew of questions at another shelter as well. Where did she plan on keeping the dog? Did she have a fence? What would happen to the dog if for some reason she could not care for it anymore?" This time, Jody was more prepared. "I had gathered all my paperwork, emailed several times, and stressed how much I was going to love Sophie and take the best care of her," she said.

Jody also explained that it's important to consider the kind of breed you're adopting, and whether the needs of that breed will fit your home and your family's lifestyle. In her application, Jody emphasized that her family was very active. The dog wouldn't be left in the house by herself; someone would be checking on her all the time and giving her ample opportunities to exercise. "I knew Border Collies, even if they are a mix, can be a bit neurotic, and they need something to do," Jody said. "They're very energetic dogs. A lot of people get Border Collies and then they can't handle them. They let them go, or they take them back to the shelter. I did a lot of research on the breed. I said whatever I could think of that might convince the shelter to give me this little dog."

The adoption process isn't always smooth sailing from the start, Jody said, and people need to be prepared for that. She admitted that once her application was approved, bringing Sophie home from the shelter was a challenge. "She was crying, she had an upset stomach, she was full of poop, and my mom and I had to bathe her, which made her cry even more," she remembered. "But we made it through that first day."

By around the third day, Sophie had fully settled into the Joyner household. "Sophie is probably the smartest dog I've ever seen," Jody told me. "She was incredible from the start. And because she's a mixed-breed dog, she has had very few health problems. Her teeth, heart, body are all great. I don't even have to worry about her overeating. She was also easy to train."

Epilogue

The roller coasters in my life have taught me that you can succeed if you never lose faith in yourself, and never give up. That doesn't mean there won't be days when you feel overwhelmed and down for the count. You just need to get back on your feet before the count reaches 10. Jesse Jackson Jr. once told me during an interview, "It's not how you fall down, but how you pick yourself up."

It's the same strength I saw with Sona. An intrepid fighting spirit was in his DNA and impressed many people, especially when he was so ill. There were times when I, or even he, might have thrown in the towel. But Sona seemed to have such determination, such faith that we were there for each other. Somehow, he always made me feel that no matter what happened, we would make it through and find ways to cope.

That fighting spirit is what often separates the winners from the losers, after all, whether you're talking about dogs or humans. How often have you heard a story about a person who gets dire medical news and says, "I'm just not going to let this beat me."

Sometimes, a dog's true grit is so impressive that he becomes a hero.

The American Humane Hero Dog Awards (www.herodogawards.org) honors dogs that have shown extraordinary devotion, bravery, and companionship. One of the most touching stories was of an emerging hero, a three-legged dog named Cassidy, who didn't seem to realize that he didn't have four legs. His zest and can-do spirit have been an inspiration for people with disabilities, showing that limitations need not diminish life or keep them from succeeding. For all of Sona's medical challenges we would never have made it alone. If you're lucky, you find people along the way that can help. Sona and I had a network of loving souls always in our corner.

Sometimes I got by on blind faith. Often when Sona was sick, I would go to St. Patrick's Cathedral in New York City and pray. Occasionally I said to God, "This is not the time for a coffee break! I need help." I remember that when Billy Graham was asked what his favorite prayer was, he would answer, "Lord, help me." There was also a pastor at New York's Fifth Avenue Presbyterian Church who told his congregation that people will often run to church to beg for God's help with a problem. But once the problem was solved, he said, very few people ever came back to say, "Thank you." I made it a point to say "thank you" as often as possible.

I thought about Sona a lot when I was working on a book titled, *Keep Going No Matter What: The Reginald F. Lewis Legacy 20 Years Later*. It is a look at an African American businessman who, in putting together a $985 million leveraged buyout of Beatrice Foods International Co., faced great obstacles but always bounced back and became a winner.

There are times when I think of all that I have endured, and then I remember Sona with love and, yes, with gratitude. Each picture of him in my apartment is a reminder of what a true friend and great dog he was—an undeniable, indefatigable winner! Everything about him was unique, from his personality, to his playfulness, to his soldiering on against the odds, to his loving spirit—all of which inspired others to believe in him and to find strength in themselves.

Sometimes, I wonder what Sona thought of me as his "mom." Did I measure up? If he could talk, what would he have said to me? Did he know how much I loved him? Did he realize what he meant to me and how much he'd changed my world? How he had embodied the best in life for me? How he truly was my hero? How he kept me going? I wonder if he knew that, in my mind, I will always remember him as smart, sassy—and, above all, a survivor.

About The Author

Ponchitta Pierce is known as a journalist, television host and producer and media consultant. She joined *Ebony* magazine as an Assistant Editor and later became New York Editor for *Ebony* and New York Bureau Chief for the magazine's then-parent company, Johnson Publishing Company. Miss Pierce worked at CBS News as a Special Correspondent and at WNBC-TV in New York, where she hosted and co-produced the daily television show *Today in New York*. She returned to the world of print as a Contributing Editor for *Parade* and *McCall's* magazines, a Roving Editor for *Reader's Digest*, and a writer for other national publications. Several of her interviews appear in the book *My Soul Looks Back in Wonder: Voices of the Civil Rights Experience* (AARP/Sterling Publishing). Miss Pierce's work is also included in the book *The Leader of the Future 2: Visions, Strategies, and Practices for the New Era*. She later conducted interviews for the book *Keep Going No Matter What: The Reginald F. Lewis Legacy 20 Years Later*.

Miss Pierce is a member of the board of trustees at WNET; the Inner-City Scholarship Fund and Morris-Jumel Mansion. She is a director of The HELP USA Fund, Inc. and the Cuban Artists Fund. Miss Pierce is also a member of the advisory board at USC Center on Public Diplomacy and a member of the Council on Foreign Relations. A graduate of the University of Southern California with a Bachelor of Arts degree in journalism, cum laude, Miss Pierce also studied at Cambridge University in England. She currently lives in New York City where she counts many dogs as her friends.

Acknowledgements

I owe so much to the wonderful, talented people who helped me bring Sona to literary life. Robert Schirmer, an author and editor, captured the essence of Sona's world and helped shape the resulting story. Journalist Nikhil Hutheesing shared valuable insight on the manuscript. Linda Langton, founder and president of Central Park South Publishing, kept telling me, "You need to bring Sona's story to readers." I would say no or tell her, "The time is not right." I wondered whether people would even be interested. I'm glad I finally listened to her.

Sona had an urban village, so to speak, and neither he nor I would have made it without the unwavering support of Maria Nikolakopoulos, my former assistant, and my friends, John and Martha Gallagher, to help take care of him. I am also deeply grateful to all the doctors who treated Sona with such care and expertise, and who often got us through some pretty rough moments.

I am from New Orleans, Louisiana; most of my family still lives there. I'm not sure they realize how much I value that they stay in touch. Finally, I remember with great fondness and appreciation all the friends who would always ask about Sona, making sure he was never forgotten, often recalling the funny things he did, and making us all laugh.

www.ingramcontent.com/pod-product-compliance
Lightning Source LLC
Chambersburg PA
CBHW071448070526
44578CB00001B/257